THE DOORS

ELEKTRA RECORDS

THE DOORS

THE COMPLETE LYRICS

Compiled by

Danny Sugerman

Delta

A Delta Book
Published by
Dell Publishing
a division of
Bantam Doubleday Dell Publishing Group, Inc.
666 Fifth Avenue
New York, New York 10103

ISBN: 0-385-30840-X

Reprinted by arrangement with Hyperion, New York, New York.

Manufactured in the United States of America

Published simultaneously in Canada

November 1992

10 9 8 7 6 5 4 3 2 1

KPH

CONTENTS

PART II

WAITING FOR THE SUN
THE SOFT PARADE

PART III

MORRISON HOTEL/HARD ROCK CAFE
L.A. WOMAN

PART IV

THE DOORS IN CONCERT
AN AMERICAN PRAYER

INTRODUCTION

BY DANNY SUGERMAN

"All you who have ardently sought to discover the laws that govern your being, who have aspired to the infinite, and whose emotions have had to seek a terrible relief in the wine of debauchery, pray for him. Now his bodily being, purified, floats amid the beings whose existence he glimpsed. Pray for him who sees and knows . . ."

—Charles Baudelaire, on Edgar Allan Poe

The Doors are somewhat of an anomaly in the rock pantheon. They weren't part of the peace 'n' love Airplane-Dead-Quicksilver acid-rock sound of San Francisco. They had nothing to do with the English invasion, or even pop music in general. While New York City was good to the Doors—almost to the point of adopting them as their own—they still weren't in league with the Velvet Underground, despite a mutual affinity for dark and somber themes. They weren't even part of Los Angeles's predominantly folk-rock scene, consisting of the Byrds, Buffalo Springfield, and the like. Even among the hierarchy that includes Elvis, Dylan, Joplin, or Hendrix, they were a world unto themselves. But what a wonderful and darkly exotic world it was.

The Doors were a band and each individual part formed a side of the diamond that was the whole. One night, on the road, just before the concert was to begin, a disc jockey climbed on the stage to introduce the act:

"Ladies and gentlemen," he announced to the audience, "please welcome Jim Morrison and the Doors." There was the customary applause.

As the DJ walked down the stairs leading from the stage, Jim pulled him aside and said, "Uh-uh, man, you go back up there and introduce us right."

The DJ panicked. "What did I say? What did I do?"

"It's *THE DOORS,*" Jim said, *"the name of the band is THE DOORS."*

When the Doors' first managers tried to lure Jim away from the rest of the group with promises of wealth and independence that a solo venture could provide, Jim immediately went over to Ray and informed him, "These two guys are trying to break up the band; let's get rid of them." The managers were bought out of their contract; from that time on, their roadie became the Doors' representative, and the four Doors essentially managed themselves. Nobody would ever again try to drive a wedge between Jim and the band, and no one would ever tell these guys what to do.

Anybody who spent any time within the charmed inner circle loosely referred to as "the Doors' Family" knew that the Doors were more than just Jim. There was no question the Doors needed Jim, and everyone knew it. They needed his dark, brilliant, raw and powerful, impulsive and explosive, elegant and refined Dionysian energy. But everyone knew that Jim needed their pristine talents, their disciplined Apollonian abilities to wrest his lyrics to music, to create the soundtrack for his profane madness and sacred inspiration. It's no mystery why Jim Morrison never went solo: He knew he needed Robby Krieger, John Densmore, and Ray Manzarek as much as they needed him.

So sympathetic were the musicians to Jim's mission that Robby Krieger was even capable of writing lyrics and songs that sounded sometimes more like Morrison than Morrison, among them "Light My Fire," "Love Me Two Times," and "Touch Me." Without Messrs. Krieger, Manzarek, and Densmore, there's a good chance Jim's songs would never have made it off the page, to say nothing of

into rehearsal, onto the stage, into the recording studio and, in defiance of all odds, across the decades.

The question arises repeatedly: Why are the Doors still so popular? Why the Doors? Why now?

Clearly, it has a lot to do with the unlikely musical elements. Robby Krieger: not only an excellent songwriter, but a fine flamenco guitarist as well, who could also play a unique kind of bottleneck guitar. Ray Manzarek: a classically trained keyboardist with a genuine love for the blues, who also wrote and played the bass lines, keeping them melodic and precise. John Densmore: a jazz drummer with an unbeatable knack for shamanic rhythm and theatrical timing. Jim Morrison: the baritone, the electric poet with an inborn compositional ability.

The combination of these diverse traits could have been disastrous, conflicting and at odds. But it wasn't. Instead it was eerie and magical, sounding like a cross between a funeral dirge and a Halloween wedding. During the first rehearsals in Manzarek's beach-front house in Venice, California, the magic was already evident to the four involved—they *knew*. None of them had ever felt like this before. There was more than a musician's innate sense of musical communication. There was chemistry. There was beauty, surrealism, and majesty. It worked.

The band's unexpressed goal was nothing short of musical alchemy—they intended to unite rock music unlike any ever heard before with poetry and that hybrid with theater and drama. They aimed to unite performer and audience by plugging directly into the Universal Mind. They would settle for nothing less. For them that meant no gimmicks, nothing up their sleeves, no elaborate staging or special effects—only naked, dangerous reality, piercing the veil of Maya with the music's ability to awaken man's own dormant eternal powers.

The Doors constantly courted their muse—that is to say, Morrison courted *his* muse, and the band followed; the band stayed with him. Jim always maintained that one cannot simply will the muse; the writer or artist's power lies in his ability to receive, not invent, and it

4

was the artist's duty to do everything possible to increase his powers of reception. To achieve this end the nineteenth-century poet Arthur Rimbaud had advocated a systematic "rational derangement of all the senses." Why? "To achieve the unknown."

Jim's fondness for the unknown is well documented. "There are things known," Jim would say in a quote often attributed to William Blake but in fact Jim's own, "and there are things unknown, and in between are the doors." But Blake did say, in his first Proverb of Hell, "The road of excess leads to the palace of wisdom." And one line down, "Prudence is a rich ugly old maid courted by Incapacity." It needn't be added that Jim did not court the maid and seldom knew incapacity. Jim drank and yelled and pleaded, cajoled and danced in honor of divine inspiration, and to hell with the cost, calling on his inspiration to unite the band, to ignite the audience, to set the night on fire, once and for all, forever.

Manzarek, Krieger, and Densmore's contribution cannot be underestimated or overpraised. For it was not only what they gave that counts for so much, but what they were willing to hold back and what they graciously sacrificed as well. It was the only way the spell could be cast, the only possible way for the songs to be born. The musicians were literally able to anticipate the singer during an improvisation, and the singer, sensing this, grew in ability and confidence. They became more daring. The Doors' muscle flexed. They were so strong they were terrifying. But in that terror was beauty, joy, and hope.

Sadly, it was the Doors' commitment to this standard, set so early in their career, that finally did them in. Jim Morrison was a man who would not, could not, and did not know how to compromise himself or his art. And herein lay his innocence and purity—his summary blessing and curse. To go all the way or die trying. All or nothing. The ecstatic risk. Because he would not manufacture or cheapen what he wrote, he could not fake desperation. He would not merely entertain, or go through the motions; he was brilliant and desperate, he was driven, he was mad—mad to create, mad to be real. And those qualities made him volatile, dangerous and conflicted. He sought consolation and solace in the same elements that had initially inspired him and helped him to create: intoxicants.

Jim Morrison was not hooked on any drug so much as he was addicted to peak experiences, specifically the high of the Doors' functioning at the pinnacle of their collective strengths, those times when muse and musician become one and the audience virtually became a part of the band. It was commitment that made this possible, and it was commitment which he refused to sacrifice.

The French Surrealist Antonin Artaud's theories regarding confrontation, as expounded in his thesis *The Theatre and Its Double*, were a significant influence on the group. In one of the book's most powerful essays, Artaud draws a parallel between the plague and theatrical action, maintaining that dramatic activity must be able to effect a catharsis in the spectator in the same way that the plague purified mankind. The goal? "So they will be terrified and awaken. I want to awaken them. They do not realize they are already dead."

Jim would, in time, scream "Wake Up!" a thousand times, a thousand nights, in an effort to shake the audience out of their self-imposed lethargy and unconsciousness. I can still remember the first Doors concert I went to, scared to the very depth of my thirteen-year-old soul, thinking: This guy is dangerous. Someone's gonna get hurt, probably him. Or me. Or all of us. When you confront that sort of fear—or the unholy terror a song like "The End" can engender—something inside you shifts. Confronting the end, eternity blinks. That concert changed my life. I knew: It doesn't get any better, or more real, than this. Today, more than twenty years later, I still feel the same way. I still don't know exactly what happened to me that night back in 1967. But I know it was transcendent.

"Mystery festivals should be unforgettable events, casting their shadows over the whole of one's future life, creating experiences that transform existence," Aristotle wrote, pointing out that the objective of the mysterium initiation, learning, was not the end, and that experiencing was the start.

Plutarch had attempted to describe the process of dying in terms

6

of a similar initiation: "Wandering astray, down frightening paths in darkness that lead nowhere; then immediately before the end of all terrible things, panic and amazement." There are magical sounds and dances and sacred words passed, and then "the initiate, set free and loose from all bondage, walks about, celebrating the festival with other sacred and pure people and he looks down on the initiated. . . ."

Which comes damn close to describing the Doors at the peak of their powers: riding the snake, the serpent, ancient and archetypal, strange yet disturbingly familiar, powerfully evocative, sensuous and evil, strong, forbidding. When Morrison intoned, "The killer awoke before dawn and put his boots on/he took a face from the ancient gallery/and he walked on down the hall," we were walking down that hall with him, in dread, paralyzed, powerless to stop, as the music wove a web of hysteria around us, wrapping us ever tighter in its web, Morrison enacting the tragedy, the patricide, the horror, unspeakable torment. WE SAW IT, WE FELT IT, we were there. We were hypnotized. Reality opened up its gaping abyss and swallowed us whole as we tumbled into another dimension. And Morrison was the only guide: "And I'm right here, I'm going to release control, we're breaking through. . . ." And then we did.

"Lost in a Roman wilderness of pain." It wasn't merely a verse. It was an epitaph for the moment, a photograph of the collective unconscious. The symbols were timeless and the words contained stored-up images and energies thousands of years old, now resurrected.

Early in the group's career, Jim tried to explain some of this to a journalist: "A Doors concert is a public meeting called by us for a special dramatic discussion. When we perform, we're participating in the creation of a world and we celebrate that with the crowd."

A few days before he flew to Paris, to his death, Jim gave his last statement to the press: "For me, it was never really an act, those so-called performances. It was a life-and-death thing; an attempt to communicate, to involve many people in a private world of thought."

It was the mid-to-late 1960s and bands were singing of love and peace and acid was passed out, but with the Doors it was different. The emerald green night world of Pan, god of music and panic, was never more resplendent than in the Doors' music: the breathless gallop in "Not to Touch the Earth," the incipient horror of "Celebration of the Lizard," the oedipal nightmare of "The End," the cacophonous torment of "Horse Latitudes," and the dark, uneasy undertones of "Can't See Your Face in My Mind," the weary doom impending in "Hyacinth House," the alluring loss of consciousness found in "Crystal Ship."

When the music was over, there was a stillness, a serenity, a connection with life and a confirmation of existence. In showing us Hell, the Doors took us to Heaven. In evoking death, they made us feel alive. By confronting us with horror, we were freed to celebrate with them joy. By confirming our sense of hopelessness and sorrow, they led us to freedom, or at least they tried.

An account of initiation into the mysteries of the goddess Isis survives in only one in-person account, an ancient text that translated reads: "I approached the frontier of death, I saw the threshold of Persephone, I journeyed through all the elements and came back, I saw at midnight the sun, sparkling in white light, I came close to the gods of the upper and the netherworld and adored them near at hand."

This all happened at night. With music and dance and performance. The concert as ritual, as initiation. The spell cast. Extraordinary elements were loosed that have resided in the ether for hundreds of thousands of years, dormant within us all, requiring only an awakening.

Of course, psychedelic drugs as well as alcohol could encourage the unfolding of events. A Greek musicologist gives his description of a Bacchic initiation as catharsis: "This is the purpose of Bacchic initiation, that the depressive anxiety of less educated people, produced by their state of life, or some misfortune, be cleared away through the melodies and dances of the ritual"

There is a strange tantalizing fascination evoked by fragments of

8

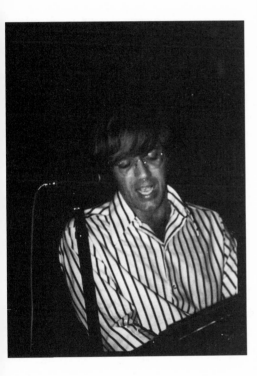

ancient pagan mysteries: The darkness and the light, the agony and the ecstasy, the sacrifice and bliss, the wine and the ear of grain (hallucinogenic fungi). For the ancients it was enough to know there were doors to a secret dimension that might open for those who earnestly sought them. Such hopes and needs have not gone away with time.

Morrison was the first rock star I know of to speak of the mythic implications and archetypal powers of rock 'n' roll, about the ritualistic properties of the rock concert. For doing so, the press called him a pretentious asshole: "Don't take yourself so seriously, Morrison, it's just rock 'n' roll and you're just a rock singer."

Jim knew they were wrong, but he didn't argue. Jim knew that music is magic, performance is worship, and he knew rhythm can set you free. Jim was too aware of the historical relevance of music in ritual for those transforming Doors concerts to have been accidental.

From Friedrich Nietzsche, Jim took solace and encouragement in the admonition to "say yes to life." I never believed that Jim was on a death trip, and to this day still find it difficult to judge the way he chose to live and die. Jim preferred intensity to longevity, to be, as Nietzsche said, "one who does not negate," who does not just say no, who dares to create himself.

Jim also must have been braced to read the following Nietzsche quote: "Saying yes to life even in its strangest and hardest problems; the will to life rejoicing over its own inexhaustibility even in the very sacrifice of its highest types—this is what I called Dionysian, that is what I understood as the bridge to the psychology of the tragic poet. Not in order to get rid of terror and pity, not in order to purge oneself of a dangerous effect by its vehement discharge, but in order to be oneself the eternal joy of becoming, beyond all terror and pity." It was Jim's insatiable thirst for life that killed him, not any love of death.

The band took their name from the poet/visionary/artist William Blake. Blake had written, "When the doors of perception are cleansed, things will appear as they truly are, infinite." English author Aldous Huxley was sufficiently inspired by Blake's quote to title his book on his mescaline experiences *The Doors of Perception*. Morrison was impressed enough with both sources to propose the monicker to his bandmates. Everyone agreed that the name, as well as the sources from which it sprang, were perfect to convey and represent who they were and what they stood for.

And then there was the first single, "Break on Through (to the Other Side)," a near-perfect distillation of what this young band was aiming to do. The imagery read like a surreal invitation to a perpetual night world with vague promises of the forbidden. The Doors were thrilling: part joy, part dread.

Nietzsche, Van Gogh, Rimbaud, Baudelaire, Poe, Blake, Artaud, Cocteau, Nijinsky, Byron, Coleridge, Dylan Thomas, Brendan Behan . . . the mad ones, the doomed ones, the writers, poets, and painters, the artists stubbornly resistant to authority and insistent on being loyal to their true nature, at any cost—this was the lineage with whom Jim most passionately identified, and it was to their standard he aspired. To be a poet, to be an artist, meant more than writing or painting or singing; it meant having a vision and the courage to see that vision through, despite any opposition. What didn't kill you made you stronger, and if you had what it took, you were rare and wondrous, and if you didn't, it couldn't be faked.

When Jim was asked by a fan mag how he prepared for stardom he answered, "I stopped getting haircuts." What he didn't say was, "and started dropping acid." Like so many others, Jim took drugs to expand his consciousness, to gain entry into worlds otherwise locked and sealed off. Aware of a shaman's relationship to his inner world via peyote, and Castaneda's experiences with Don Juan, Jim ingested psychedelics. Like Coleridge and the opium eaters, he was held spellbound by the artificial paradise, the hypnagogic architecture, the milky seas and starless nights. As with Huxley, Jim marveled before the splendiferous geometry and ancient secrets trembling on the verge of revelation. And like the romantic poets, he reveled in the altering of his senses with anything available—wine, hash, whiskey. . . . If absinthe had been around, Morrison would have been an absinthe drinker. In *The Varieties of Religious Experience*, William James wrote what Jim already knew: "Sobriety diminishes, discriminates, and says no; drunkenness expands, unites, and says yes." And when the visions no longer pleased or surprised him, when intoxication no longer provided him with the expansive awareness he sought, as Dionysus, the god of ecstasy, became Bacchus, the representative for drunkenness, Jim turned more and more to alcohol to numb the pain and to revel in unconsciousness.

At first he drank for the pure joy of it. "I enjoy drinking," he admitted. "It loosens people up and stimulates conversation. Somehow it's like gambling; you go out for a night of drinking, and you don't know where you'll end up the next morning. It could be good, could be a disaster, it's a throw of the dice. The difference between suicide and slow capitulation."

And at the end he got drunk for the simple reason that that is what alcoholics do.

To be a poet meant more than writing poems. It demanded a commitment to live and die with great style and even greater sadness; to wake each morning with the fever raging and know it would never be extinguished except by death. To be a poet meant making a commitment. To embrace the tragedy fate has chosen for you and fulfill that destiny with gusto and nobility.

And now, twenty years after Jim's death, the Morrison/Doors story has blossomed into the realm of myth. Jim's short tragic life is the stuff of which our heroes and our gods of youth and resurrection are made. Like Orpheus, he is forever young, and like Dionysus, he dies to be born again. And as with the murder of Adonis, the sacrifice of Mithra, and the accidental death of Antinous, he could not have lived without destroying the myth on which his audience has founded itself. One of the reasons Jim went to Paris was that he could no longer live up to the mythology he himself had helped create.

Osiris proclaimed, "My hair is the hair of Nu; my eyes are the eyes of Hathor; my neck is the neck of the divine goddess Isis." And Morrison, too, is a composite of deities who traversed the world before: the hair and the inclination of the neck of Alexander the Great; the slouch from Marlon Brando; the hooded eyes of James Dean; the torment of Montgomery Clift; the behavior and attitude of Rimbaud; the voice of Sinatra; the radiance of the young Elvis Presley . . . And then he changed from the beautiful Adonis to the bearded and fatherly Zeus.

But Jim Morrison didn't want to be a god. Jim Morrison wanted to be a poet.

There is a popular theory circulating among certain intellectual groups and around psychological circles these days that our Apollonian abilities, our rational minds have far outdistanced our Dionysian needs and the result is a psychic rupture in the fabric of our collective unconscious. Our productive twentieth-century minds have created comforts and computers at a disastrous cost to our psychic nature, our spiritual needs. A similar imbalance was addressed during England's industrial revolution when the romantic poets Byron, Keats, and Shelley rose to fame and infamy, "wantons, infidels, seducers all," extolling the virtues of indulgence.

No modern poet has written better of the alienation and feelings of isolation, dread, and disconnectedness than Jim Morrison. We've been walled-in, malled-in, insulated, air-conditioned, cine-plexed, programmed, brainwashed, unalterably directed by materialism, consumerism, and capitalism, unaware of our own heartbeats, only dimly aware of our diminished, starving spirits. The Doors and Morrison told us what it was really like. "People are strange, when you're a stranger," Morrison wrote, "faces look ugly when you're alone. Women seem wicked when you're unwanted. Streets are uneven when you're down."

Jim was aware of this modern schism, this sense of dislocation, our angst: "If my poetry aims to achieve anything, it's to deliver people from the limited ways in which they see and feel."

When asked at a European press conference how he would describe the Doors' music, a drunk and jet-lagged Jim described it like this: "The feeling I get is a kind of heavy, sort of gloomy feeling, like of someone not quite home, or not quite relaxed . . . aware of a lot of things but not quite sure about anything . . . I'd like to do one just . . . um . . . of being totally at home."

Before freedom is achieved, before one arrives home, first you must be lost, wandering, devoid of hope; first you have to traverse the abyss. Before the dawn by necessity comes the relentless night, what St. John of the Cross called "the dark night of the soul," and Dante referred to as "the Dark Wood." It is a mandatory chapter of the hero's journey. And it's this path the true artist must travel. Inching up to the abyss compelled Rimbaud to write, "I have felt the wing of madness pass over me." Baudelaire fought with the chilling and terrible winds emanating from the same depths when he wrote, "The wind of fear has made my blood run cold."

In a poem titled simply "The Abyss," Baudelaire tries to describe the wordless horror, the indifferent void. Sartre called this pit "No Exit" for a reason—because no one here gets out alive. "Some are born to sweet delight," Jim wrote, "and some are born to the endless night." And there was no doubt as to where Jim had been spending the majority of his time. Morrison called to us his sightings and invited us to join him, but we couldn't, and he couldn't wait. And he wouldn't take a step backwards or alter his fate. Knowing the cost, knowing the risks but driven by his insatiable thirst to see all, feel all, and do everything, Jim ran up to the edge of that abyss and found a freedom so complete and vast it was terrifying. And then he dove in.

I don't believe Jim's goal, his ambition, his ultimate destination was this dark place. I think Jim wanted enlightenment. But Jim knew that the road of excess leading to the palace of wisdom is fraught with despair and disaster as much as with ecstasy and great joy. And that despair must not be suppressed but experienced, and only then may it be discarded.

Jim's dying wish was to be taken seriously as a poet. While he was alive, his behavior blinded many of us to his words. Today his life still fascinates and amazes us, but his work as a poet can now stand alone.

During his lifetime, Morrison had been compared to an angel and called the devil, and almost everything in between. From Mephistofeles to the ultimate Barbie doll, from the King of Acid Rock to Mickey Mouse de Sade. The conflicts raged within. He sought immortality as a poet only to see those efforts sabotaged by his enormous appeal as a rock star. Still, Jim got what he wanted. Jim wanted to be like a shooting star; now you see him, now you don't. Jim wanted to transubstantiate the temporal energy and light of life into the lasting immortality of art. What he hadn't counted on was that the impact he made would last so long. I think he'd be pleased—I think he'd be proud.

And in the end, after conquering America and the rest of the Western world, after being shackled by the courts and laws of the land that he loved, he escaped to Paris, home of so many expatriate artists of the past, to further his life as a poet. But his body was too worn down, his heart too weak; he had already seen and done and drunk too much. He had lived life on his terms, he had reaped the rewards, and now the bill was due. His spirit was tired. Death was simply closer and easier than returning to America, or the stage it represented.

Jim Morrison is not dead. His spirit lives on, in his music and in these lyrics, shining with incandescent brilliance, a fusion of light and dark made diamond bright and eternal.

"Cancel my subscription to the resurrection," he sang.

Not likely, Jim.

This is not the end.

PART I

THE DOORS
STRANGE DAYS

PERCEIVING THE DOORS

BY PAUL NELSON

The following piece is resurrected from the long out-of-print songbook We Are the Doors. *It serves as a literate and appropriate introduction to the Doors, combining biographical material culled from the group's first Elektra Records bio, original insights on the part of the writer, and quotes from band members.*

It has become a standard practice, when writing about the Doors, to begin each article with a eulogy concerning their demonic powers. All those D's, I suppose, bring out the Devil in both the Doors and the diarists. It's easy enough to do: You simply cast Morrison as a rock Faust (or even a possessed Jesus Christ) and you're halfway home.

I've done it myself: "And Jim. To see him sing is like witnessing a man dangling in some kind of unique and personal pain. Watching Morrison come face to face with some ultimate truth in song can be truly frightening. The shrieks and screams come from a subconscious layer under the conscious artistry: Morrison is levels, not all of them pretty."

Here is my favorite Doors "demon" story. Nipper Holzman (small son of Jac, the president of Elektra, the record company for which the Doors record) once announced, when we were all sitting around listening to *Strange Days,* that the Doors were creatures from another planet who came here to change our music. Everyone laughed, but it was a laughter in the dark as we heard the sounds of "People Are Strange" and "When the Music's Over" ooze and glide and unwind off of the phonograph and into our consciousness.

I suppose that the point of all of this is neither to prove nor to disprove the manic mythology of the music of Morrison, Manzarek, Krieger, and Densmore, but merely to show that the handling of such melodramatic and impressionistic matters can be either childish or childlike—and that not too much attention should be paid to it. People tend to forget that the Doors are musicians, too. Since this is a guide to their music, let us not make that mistake.

Without getting too technical, what characterizes the Doors, individually and as a group musically? What about *that* sound?

First, let's describe it impressionistically. (Have you seen the Doors "live"?) When they play, they seem to be held together by both terrific, almost terrifying, strength and by sheer nervous tension. They expand, contract, and the song is stretched like a live thing to a point of birth or breaking or both. The passion is always contained within the control. Ray plays the organ like a holy man, his thoughts almost as visible as smoke, while Robby oozes out those slow, melted flamenco notes as if he were shaking them from a slow-motion guitar. John is all speed and power on the drums, a perpetual-motion machine. And Jim. To see him sing is like witnessing . . .

Then, a break on through to the other side: "realism." The basic sound of the Doors emanates from Ray Manzarek's staccato yet melodic organ. Here, a great deal of the rhythmic foundation of the music is laid, since the group does not use a bass. Manzarek is an action organist in that he uses the technique of attacking the instrument in his playing of it (although nothing about his artistry ever seems forced or frantic: quite the opposite). John Densmore's expressionistic use of drums is also unique, with its stress on dramatic texture rather than on pure rhythm, on accents rather than on a heavy

beat. He works closely with words and not riffs, carrying on a dialogue with the lyrics.

The Doors are primarily an instrumental trio with a lead singer, but Jim Morrison is not so much a singer per se as he is a shouter, as horn section, sometimes a lead instrument. He doesn't sing in the dictionary sense of the word; rather, he *punctuates* with his voice. Tying all of the elements together—the organ, the drums, the vocals—is the fluid thread of Robby Krieger's guitar, slow, spare, thoughtful, unifying. Krieger's thought processes for guitar, interestingly enough, did not come from blues but from flamenco, a fact that makes his guitar playing totally individualistic in the rock field.

Jim once told a reporter: "We're the Doors because, when you go into a strange town, you check into a hotel. Then, after you've played your gig, you go back to your room, down an endless corridor lined with doors, until you get to your own. But, when you open the door, you find there are lots of people inside. And you wonder, Am I in the wrong room? Or is this some kind of a party?"

Yes, the Doors are mystical (hailing from Los Angeles, to preserve their sanity, perhaps they have to be). But they can talk common sense, too. Here is Robby: "Most groups today aren't groups. Here, we use everyone's ideas. In a true group, all of the members create the arrangements among themselves. This group is so serious. It's the most serious group that ever was, that ever will be." And Ray: "All of us have the freedom to explore and to improvise within a framework. Jim is an improviser with words. . . . We've all shattered ourselves a long time ago. That was what early rock was about: an attempt to shatter two thousand years of culture. Now, we're working on what happens after you've shattered it."

Perhaps this statement by Jim best marries the mythological and the matter-of-fact: "You could say it's an accident that I was ideally suited for the work I am doing. It's the feeling of a bow string being pulled back for twenty-two years and suddenly being let go. . . . I've always been attracted to ideas that were about revolt against authority.

When you make your peace with authority, you become an authority. I like ideas about the breaking away or overthrowing of established order. I am interested in anything about revolt, disorder, chaos, especially activity which seems to have no meaning. It seems to me to be the road toward freedom—external revolt is a way to bring about internal freedom. Rather than starting inside, I start outside—reach the mental through the physical. But the main thing is that we are the Doors. We are from the West. The world we suggest should be of a new, wild West, a sensuous, evil world, strange and haunting. The path of the sun, you know.''

ELEKTRA RECORDS

THE DOORS

All songs written and arranged by the Doors
All lyrics by Jim Morrison except as otherwise noted

BREAK ON THROUGH

You know the day destroys the night
Night divides the day
Tried to run
Tried to hide
Break on through to the other side
Break on through to the other side
Break on through to the other side

We chased our pleasures here
Dug our treasures there
Can you still recall
The time we cried?
Break on through to the other side
Break on through to the other side
Break on through to the other side

Ev'rybody loves my baby
Ev'rybody loves my baby

She gets, she gets
She gets, she gets

I found an island in your arms
A country in your eyes
Arms that chained us
Eyes that lied
Break on through to the other side
Break on through to the other side
Break on through to the other side

Made the scene from week to week
Day to day, hour to hour
The gate is straight
Deep and wide
Break on through to the other side
Break on through to the other side
Break on through to the other side

Break on through, break on through
Break on through, break on through

Yeah, yeah, yeah,
Yeah, yeah, yeah . . .

SOUL KITCHEN

Well, the clock says it's time
   to close now
I guess I'd better go now
I'd really like to stay here all night

The cars crawl past all stuffed
   with eyes
Street lights shed their hollow glow
Your brain seems bruised with
   numb surprise

Still one place to go
Still one place to go

Let me sleep all night in your
   soul kitchen
Warm my mind near your gentle stove
Turn me out and I'll wander, baby
Stumbling in the neon groves

Your fingers weave quick minarets
Speak in secret alphabets
I light another cigarette
Learn to forget, learn to forget
Learn to forget, learn to forget

Let me sleep all night in your
   soul kitchen
Warm my mind near your gentle stove
Turn me out and I'll wander, baby
Stumbling in the neon groves

Well, the clock says it's time
   to close now
I know I have to go now
I really want to stay here all night
All night
All night

JOSEPH SIA

THE CRYSTAL SHIP

Before you slip into unconsciousness
I'd like to have another kiss
Another flashing chance at bliss
Another kiss
Another kiss

The days are bright and
    filled with pain
Enclose me in your gentle rain
The time you ran was too insane
We'll meet again
We'll meet again

Oh tell me where your freedom lies
The streets are fields that never die
Deliver me from reasons why
You'd rather cry
I'd rather fly

The crystal ship is being filled
A thousand girls, a thousand thrills
A million ways to spend your time
When we get back
I'll drop a line

TWENTIETH CENTURY FOX

Well, she's fashionably lean
And she's fashionably late
She'll never rank a scene
She'll never break a date
But she's no drag
Just watch the way she walks

She's a twentieth century fox
She's a twentieth century fox

No tears, no fears
No ruined years
No clocks
She's a twentieth century fox

She's the queen of cool
And she's the lady who waits
Since her mind left school
It never hesitates
She won't waste time
On elementary talk

'Cause she's a twentieth century fox
She's a twentieth century fox

Got the world locked up
Inside a plastic box
She's a twentieth century fox, oh yeah
Twentieth century fox, oh yeah
Twentieth century fox
She's a twentieth century fox

LIGHT MY FIRE

Lyrics by Robby Krieger and Jim Morrison

You know that it would be untrue
You know that I would be a liar
If I was to say to you
Girl, we couldn't get much higher

Come on, baby, light my fire
Come on, baby, light my fire
Try to set the night on fire

The time to hesitate is through
No time to wallow in the mire
Try now we can only lose
And our love become a funeral pyre

Come on, baby, light my fire
Come on, baby, light my fire
Try to set the night on fire

The time to hesitate is through
No time to wallow in the mire
Try now we can only lose
And our love become a funeral pyre

Come on, baby, light my fire
Come on, baby, light my fire
Try to set the night on fire

You know that it would be untrue
You know that I would be a liar
If I was to say to you
Girl, we couldn't get much higher

Come on, baby, light my fire
Come on, baby, light my fire
Try to set the night on fire

Try to set the night on fire
Try to set the night on fire
Try to set the night on fire

I LOOKED AT YOU

I looked at you
You looked at me
I smiled at you
You smiled at me

And we're on our way
No, we can't turn back
Yeah, we're on our way
And we can't turn back
'Cause it's too late
Too late, too late
Too late, too late

And we're on our way
No, we can't turn back
Yeah, we're on our way
And we can't turn back

I walked with you
You walked with me
I talked to you
You talked to me

And we're on our way
No, we can't turn back
Yeah, we're on our way
And we can't turn back
'Cause it's too late
Too late, too late
Too late, too late

And we're on our way
No, we can't turn back
Yeah, we're on our way
And we can't turn back
'Cause it's too late
Too late, too late
Too late, too late

END OF THE NIGHT

Take the highway to the
   end of the night
End of the night
End of the night
Take a journey to the bright midnight
End of the night
End of the night

Realms of bliss
Realms of light
Some are born to sweet delight
Some are born to sweet delight
Some are born to the endless night

End of the night
End of the night
End of the night
End of the night

Realms of bliss
Realms of light
Some are born to sweet delight
Some are born to sweet delight
Some are born to the endless night

End of the night
End of the night
End of the night
End of the night

JOSEPH SIA

TAKE IT AS IT COMES

Time to live
Time to lie
Time to laugh
Time to die

Take it easy, baby
Take it as it comes
Don't move too fast if you want your
    love to last
You've been movin' much too fast

Time to walk
Time to run
Time to aim your arrows
At the sun

Take it easy, baby
Take it as it comes
Don't move too fast if you want your
    love to last
You've been movin' much too fast

Go real slow
You'll like it more and more
Take it as it comes
Specialize in havin' fun

Take it easy, baby
Take it as it comes
Don't move too fast if you want your
    love to last
You've been movin' much too fast
Movin' much too fast
Movin' much too fast

CHUCK BOYD

THE END

This is the end, beautiful friend
This is the end, my only friend
The end of our elaborate plans
The end of ev'rything that stands
The end

No safety or surprise
The end
I'll never look into your eyes again

Can you picture what will be
So limitless and free
Desperately in need of some
    stranger's hand
In a desperate land

Lost in a Roman wilderness of pain
And all the children are insane
All the children are insane
Waiting for the summer rain
There's danger on the edge of town
Ride the king's highway
Weird scenes inside the gold mine
Ride the highway West, baby

Ride the snake
Ride the snake
To the lake
To the lake

The ancient lake, baby
The snake is long
Seven miles
Ride the snake

He's old
And his skin is cold
The West is the best
The West is the best
Get here and we'll do the rest

The blue bus is calling us
The blue bus is calling us
Driver, where are you taking us?

The killer awoke before dawn
He put his boots on

CHUCK BOYD

36

He took a face from the
    ancient gallery
And he walked on down the hall

He went into the room where his
    sister lived
And then he paid a visit to his brother
And then he walked on down the hall
And he came to a door
And he looked inside
Father?
Yes, son?
I want to kill you
Mother, I want to . . .

Come on, baby, take a chance with us
Come on, baby, take a chance with us
Come on, baby, take a chance with us
And meet me at the back of the
    blue bus

This is the end, beautiful friend
This is the end, my only friend
The end

It hurts to set you free
But you'll never follow me

The end of laughter and soft lies
The end of nights we tried to die

This is the end

GLORIA STAVERS

THE NIGHT ON FIRE:
ROTHCHILD SPEAKS

A longer version of the following article originally ran in Crawdaddy *magazine shortly after the first Doors album appeared. Editor Paul Williams wrote frequently and eloquently about the Doors. Here he speaks with the Doors' record producer, Paul Rothchild, who worked with the band from the first LP until their fifth,* Morrison Hotel.

ROCK IS ROCK:
A DISCUSSION OF A DOORS SONG

Very few people have the balls to talk about "rock and roll" anymore. *Revolver* made it difficult. *Between the Buttons, Smile,* and the Doors lp are making it impossible. "Pop music" is definable only by pointing at a current chart; the Doors are not "pop," they are simply "modern music." The term applies not because rock has achieved the high standards of mainstream music, but conversely because rock has *absorbed* mainstream music, has become the leader, the arbiter of quality, the music of today. The Doors, Brian Wilson, the Stones *are* modern music, and contemporary "jazz" and "classical" composers must try to measure up.

The Doors is an album of magnitude. Thanks to the calm surefootedness of the group, the producer, the record company, there are no flaws; the Doors have been delivered to the public full grown (by current standards) and still growing (standards change). Gestation may have been long and painful; no one cares. The birth of the group is in this album, and it's as good as anything in rock. The awesome fact about the Doors is that they will improve.

So much for the review. This record is too good to be "explained," note by note, song by song; that sort of thing could only be boring, since the review would be immediately compared to the far-more-than-merely-communicative level of the work of art itself. Knowing that my reader is able to stop after any word I write and listen to all of "Light My Fire" before reading the next word, I should feel pretty foolish offering him a textual description of the buildup of erotic pressure in the performance. Is there really any point in saying something like, "The instrumental in 'Light My Fire' builds at the end into a truly visual orgasm in sound" when the reader can at any time put the album onto even the crummiest phonograph and experience that orgasm himself? Descriptive criticism is almost a waste of time, where quality is involved. It might be more valid for a reviewer to make a comment like: "The 'come' sequence at the end of 'Light My Fire' is the most powerfully controlled release of accumulated instrumental kineticism known on record, making even 'I'm a Man' by the Yardbirds a mere firecracker," but where that may make good reading and even makes pretty good writing under ordinary circumstances, in the context of an album as great and implicational and able-to-change-history as this one, comments like that dissatisfy and bore the reviewer, because to him they're simply obvious. . . .

Anyway, I've been thinking about "Blowin' in the Wind." A lot of people misunderstand that song, and it really is [Bob] Dylan's fault. He shoved in lines like "How many times will the cannonballs fly," etc., which must have been practically *intended* to throw people off the track of what was being said. The line, "The answers my friends are blowin' in the wind" is so perfect that I doubt that anyone could hear it and not feel what is really being said (in fact, it's impossible to hear any true statement and not feel it correctly, although you may then go ahead and interpret it all wrong). But I'm not suggesting that the verses to "Blowin' " should have backed up the theme of the chorus line. The cumulative boredom that builds to a head and causes the creation of a line like "The answers are blowin' in the wind" (or, as we shall see, "Learn to forget") could not possibly then sustain the creation of an entire three verses or so of equal genius. Besides, three verses of equal genius would destroy the impact. . . .

"Soul Kitchen" is so reminiscent of "Blowin' in the Wind" in terms of message that one almost expects Peter Paul & Mary to make it a Top 40 smash. It's just a nice little song about desire, a routine drama in which Jim points out that it looks like it's time for him to go (beautiful posturing: twiddling of thumbs, glance at the clock, well, um, looks like it's time for me to leave, uh . . .) but he'd "really like to stay here all night." And he does stay, and the Doors do their usual "boy gets girl" instrumental routine, and then Jim lampoons his own posturing, repeating, "The clock says it's time to close now," but then saying, "I *know* I've got to go now." "I'd really like to stay here *all night*" changes from effective plea into bitter irony; the words that meant "let me in" before mean "sorry, baby" after. And that's almost all there is to it, except that the plea "Let me sleep all night in your soul kitchen" is so fantastically strong. Jim obviously didn't give that much of a damn about the girl in this case, so something else must have been bothering him. The intensity of that plea could not have been faked. And this leads us to the really stunning revelation that sexual desire is merely a particular instance of some more far-reaching grand dissatisfaction.

The message of "Soul Kitchen" is of course "Learn to forget," a "message"/phrase at least as powerful as "The answers my friends are blowin' in the wind" and very similar in the sort of implications and emotions it conjures up. The actual words "learn to forget" are repeated four times at the end of the second verse of "Soul Kitchen," and are never returned to in any way. In fact, the band seems to be unaware of them, and Robby [Krieger] has been known to say that he considers the piece inconsequential! And as compared with the Dylan song, a great deal of the success of this one is due to the fact that the

CHUCK BOYD

playing, and the words of the song other than "learn to forget," are almost totally unrelated to the message, and as a result they serve as emphasis rather than confusion. So this truth is totally accessible to anyone listening to the song—and the irony here is that the song is not a single, not a huge airplay hit, not being heard by more than maybe 20,000 people. (Well, the album turned out to be a #1 smash, so revise that upwards by a couple of decimal points . . .)

"Learn to forget"—what power that phrase has! It's possible to get stoned for days listening to this song . . . for a while it will seem the one truth available to us. It eventually recedes, of course, into merely a tantalizing command: Within the song it's a posthypnotic suggestion to the girl being seduced, it's a bitter comment on the necessity of learning to forget in order to get along in this grubby world, it's a statement of faith in the ability of man to will what he doesn't want out of existence. Above all, it's an echo of the Sopho-clean section of "The End" (echo because the album is programmed circularly for repeated listenings), in which it becomes necessary to kill the father. As Paul Rothchild says in *Crawdaddy!* 10, " 'Kill the fa-ther' means kill all of those things within yourself that are instilled in you and are not of yourself." Obviously, "Learn to forget," which comes from the mouth of the same man, could easily have the same meaning to Jim [Morrison]. But "The End," which is a truly beauti-ful, perfected, polished intellectual statement, cannot communicate as powerfully as "Soul Kitchen," since the latter is not on an intel-lectual level at all. "The End" is great to listen to when you're high (or any other time), but "Soul Kitchen" will get you high, which is obviously much cruder and more important. "Soul Kitchen," with its revelation that sexual desire is more complexly motivated than we think (all right, suppose it's immediately caused by the animal instinct for survival through reproduction of the self; the implications of *that* are that sexual desire is within each person that individual's expression of the agony of being and the relationship between man and the fu-ture, that is to say, the meaning of life. If I want that girl because deep down I want to assure my own survival through descendants,

44

then that look in my eyes reflects all the pain of the question: Why do I want descendants, why does man consider time a rival he must conquer? That makes sexual need [as opposed to lust] the purest form of spiritual pain known to man, and therefore the most beautiful thing around), and its fantastically ambiguous "learn to forget" . . . "Soul Kitchen," because it conjures up this kind of stuff, is a catalyst with more potential for generating truth—in my opinion—than anything since middle Faulkner.

It's important now to realize that the "the answers my friends are blowin' in the wind" phrase itself has as much potential for truth generation, within the right context, as "learn to forget." The greater value of "Soul Kitchen," which happens to contain the latter, has something to do with the triumph of rock. Rock, which is less cognitive, allows the creator of the vehicle for the phrase more freedom in subject. "Folk" basically demands a relationship between all words and ideas in a song, unless nonsense words are used, whereas rock may be as totally noncognitive without being nonsense as "Hey ninety-eight point six the love that was the medicine that saved me, oh I love my baby." Rock gave Jim Morrison the freedom to slip "learn to forget" into the middle of a seduction song, which offers no distraction at all, whereas Dylan in order to even *say* that the answers are blowing in the wind had to provide some representative questions. "Soul Kitchen" has the further advantage, common in rock, that you can't hear all the words, so you can pretty much contextualize as you like. And the direct appeal to the mind made by "folk" (straightforward words, guitar, voice) cannot compare, it seems to me, with the abilities of rock to move people's muscles, bodies, caught up and swaying and moving so that a phrase like "learn to forget" can actually become your whole body, can sink into your soul on a more-than-cognitive level. Rock, because of the number of senses it can get to (on a dance floor, eyes, ears, nose, mouth, and tactile) and the extent to which it can pervade those senses, is really the most advanced art form we have.

This interview was taped in Englewood, New Jersey, in March 1967, shortly after the release of the first Doors album, which Paul Rothchild produced. Last names are used throughout to avoid ambiguity.

WILLIAMS: Tell me about the history of the group.

ROTHCHILD: I actually know very little. I know that Ray Manzarek and Jim Morrison started performing together when they were both students at the film school at UCLA. They were friends from the film department and they found out they both had an interest in music and they started to perform. Their early music was mostly blues, with Ray doing a tremendous amount of singing.

WILLIAMS: Did Jim play anything at that time?

ROTHCHILD: No. And I don't even know where Robby [Krieger] came from or how he fitted into the group. I've never really been tremendously interested myself in the past social-musical activities of groups. The questions I usually ask musicians are about their musical past, their training, what their influences are, where they get their reasons, their musical reasons. As for where they came from and how they got together, they did all get together at the University of California at Los Angeles, and, well, they were playing together as long ago as about two and a half years, I guess. As the Doors they've been playing together for a little over a year now, a year and a half . . . And it's, uh, a constantly changing and moving process for them.

It's a relief for them to have this first album out because it gives them an opportunity to move on towards music and musical concepts that they've been discussing and wanting to get into. This is a very interesting thing that a lot of groups have, the effect that making albums has on them, and how it's almost an insistence that they change their repertoire. It's like a group goes into a recording studio and that giant performance mirror, the tape recorder, is put in front of them, they finally work out all of the problems and all of the fine

points in the music that they've been wanting to for so long, and then when they get through with the tunes a great many of them fall by the wayside. The statement's been made.

WILLIAMS: The material's never as good as on the first album for a lot of groups.

ROTHCHILD: That's right. And it's almost a kind of catharsis for the musicians to make their first album because it frees them, in many respects; it allows them to go to the other places they've been wanting to for so long but they've been tied down to their original material. This may sound strange to use words like "tied down" but it's really true; now the Doors, since they are a creative and performing group, are forced—and they enjoy it—to look forward to their next album. That means we have to get on to the new material. That doesn't mean they stop performing the old stuff; the best of it remains in the repertoire . . .

WILLIAMS: Which are the earliest songs on the album?

ROTHCHILD: "I Looked at You" and "Take It as It Comes." Those represent probably the genesis of the group, more than any others. The newer of the tunes are the ones that are deeper, the ones that show a greater maturity. "The End" is newer. "The End," it's interesting, "The End" was always a changing piece. Jim used it as a . . . almost an open canvas for his poetic bits and pieces and fragments and images and little couplets and things that he just wanted to say, and it changed all the time, it was a changing thing. Now it rarely changes. Now that it's on record and the musicians can listen to it on record it is the statement they wanted to make and Jim tends to perform it that way. Sometimes he'll leave something out, sometimes he will put something else in but now it's a formed piece, it isn't that open canvas any more. And because of this, Jim commented to me recently, the thing he's most deeply concerned with right now is opening another canvas of that nature, something as broad in concept as "The End."

WILLIAMS: On interpreting "The End": I considered for the first time the other day that the lines "This is the end, my only friend" and particularly "It hurts to set you free but you'll never follow me"—it occurred to me, when I heard that, that the song might be

GLORIA STAVERS

about a murder, and not just a guy leaving a girl. The possibility opened that the whole thing was the murderer's mind and ah, the stream of consciousness starting from and leading back *to* . . .

ROTHCHILD: It's interesting that you say that, because Jim is fascinated with the concept of death. He's interested in spiritual deaths, conceptual deaths, more than physical deaths actually; you'll find this theme in many of his songs: the line "The end of nights we tried to die . . ."

WILLIAMS: That goes right back to "Crystal Ship."

ROTHCHILD: Exactly.

I'm not sure if this is what Jim has in mind, but it's almost as if Jim is saying . . . realize this is my interpretation and not Jim's, 'cause I've never asked Jim; he presented it to me and said it's for your head, interpret it as you will, Jim's saying almost as a friend, okay, my friend and I take an acid trip, and then I say to my friend this is the end my friend, my only friend, the end of laughter and soft lies, the end of nights we tried to die, ah, the line, the end of nights we tried to die, to my mind is a direct reference to the concept that most psychedelics are a form of physical poisoning, that chemicals are a means of re-orienting the body through a kind of poison . . .

WILLIAMS: You're saying this is the end, during the trip or before it?

ROTHCHILD: The way I feel it, the trip has started and he's saying this is the end.

WILLIAMS: As a beginning.

ROTHCHILD: Right. This is the end. He has had a realization concerning a relationship; now this can be far more universal than a statement to this theoretical friend who is right there; this could be the end of the world, the end of laughter and soft lies, or the end of—

WILLIAMS: Himself.

ROTHCHILD: Precisely. He's saying okay here's a trip, every time we take a trip there's a death—of concepts, of bullshit, a death of laughter and soft lies, let's get real with ourselves, let's get real with

ROGER CORBIN

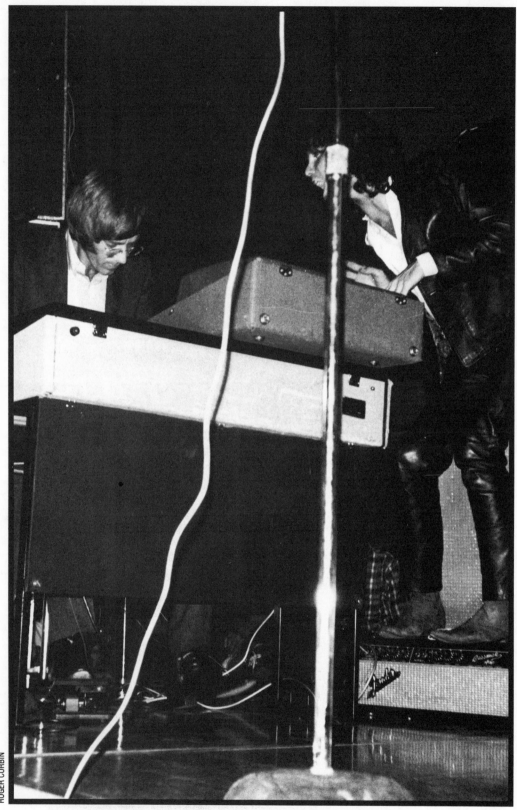

each other, um . . . there's one thing Jim used to say during the song which is just a stark death image. It was the blue bus theory, but it was stated in a different way, and he used to use them both, he used the blue bus thing and he'd also say, uh, "Have you seen the accident outside, seven people took a ride and something something something and seven people died," which is really very groovy, "have you seen the accident outside"—the world—seven people took a ride, this trip, looked at the world, and died. All of that they saw in themselves which before lived, in other words the bullshit concept of the world which had been burned into their brains since childhood, had to die. And with every end there is a beginning, it is a cyclical thing, the end always has in it inherent a beginning, uh, trying to remember . . . "Can you picture what will be so limitless and free, desperately in need of some stranger's hand in a desperate land." Things are very wrong out there, so let us kill ourselves or those things in ourselves that are false, that are bullshit, the false giddiness, the TV giddiness, canned audience reaction laughter—there's more humor in the world than needs to be created scientifically in a TV studio, I'm babbling I understand but I'm on as much of a hunch trying to explain as Jim is who's trying to lay it down.

Of the other imagery in the song, the little poetic bits between the double verse section in the beginning and the double verse section in the end, you have things like the snake—well there he's saying just get down to reality, the snake thing of course is just pure sexual imagery (to my mind), ride the snake to the ancient lake, that comes right out of Negro imagery, blues imagery, which Jim is very familiar with, "the snake he's old and his skin is cold," what he is saying is okay let's get down to the realities of life, there are very few realities and one of the few truly real realities is sexual awareness and companionship, Jim is very lucid in that department. . . . Oh right, and the first one which is very beautiful, "lost in a Roman"—oh, a piece of beautiful classical imagery—"lost in a Roman wilderness of pain." To my mind all I can see is great crumbling ruins of a great civilization, which of course flashes right back to now, "lost in a Roman wilderness of pain and all the children are insane," repeated.

WILLIAMS: The barbarians.

ROTHCHILD: Right. "Waiting for the summer rain," let's get cleansed, let's get cleansed, people. Another symbolic death by the way. Insanity of course is a symbolic death, it's a death itself, and the cleansing is a rebirth. And then of course there's the incredible Oedipal thing in the middle which is the first giant build, and I have talked with Jim about that, because I have rarely been as impressed . . .

I have never been as moved in a recording studio as I was when that take went down. I was impressed by the fact that for one of the very first times in rock-and-roll history sheer drama had taken place on tape. This to me is very important, and it's also significant that Jim has used, chose to use, a purely classical image (in modern dress) to do this. The story he tells is basically the Oedipus legend. The killer awoke before dawn, he put his boots on, he chose a face from the ancient gallery and he walked on down the hall. And he came to a door and he walked inside, and he went to the room where his brother lived, and then he went into the room where his sister lived, and then walked on down the hall, and he came to a door and he walked inside and he said, father, yes son, I want to kill you, and then he walked—

WILLIAMS: No, no, it just immediately becomes mother . . .

ROTHCHILD: Yes, there's a little musical thing and then he says mother I want to and then he screams. He screams for obvious reasons, there are even for Jim cultural limitations.

WILLIAMS: And it's more effective.

ROTHCHILD: Of course, it's more effective, it's basic, it's primal, it's the reason, it's the motivation. Jim is saying, and Jim has phrased it precisely this way, kill the father, fuck the mother, and at one point Jim said to me during the recording session, he was very emotionally moved, and he was wondering, and he was tearful, and he shouted in the studio. "Does *anybody* understand me?" And I said yes I do, and

right then and there we got into a long discussion about just what does this mean, this section, and Jim just kept saying over and over, kill the father, fuck the mother, and essentially it boils down to just this, kill the father means kill all of those things in yourself which are instilled in you and are not of yourself; they are not your own, they are alien concepts which are not yours, they must die, those are the things that must die. The psychedelic revolution. Fuck the mother is very basic, and it means get back to the essence, what is the reality, what is, fuck the mother is very basically mother, mother-birth, real, very real, you can touch it, you can grab it, you can feel it, it's nature, it's real, it can't lie to you.

So what he says at the end of the Oedipus section, which is essentially the same thing that the classic says, he is saying, kill the alien concepts, get back to reality, which is precisely what the song is about, the end, the end of alien concepts, the beginning of personal concepts. Get to reality, get to your *own* reality, get to your *own* in-touch-with-yourself situation . . .

WILLIAMS: What are the details of the sessions on this album—that is, how it went, walking into the studios for the first time.

ROTHCHILD: I'll tell you exactly. They had done a demo for Columbia and then I went to work with them for Elektra, preparing them. This is something I like to do with what I consider to be new groups, virgin groups, who have not been in studios before, because there are all kinds of problems that have to be resolved with groups before they can get down to the business of making phonograph records comfortably. The common concept for recording studios—which is not mine—is that recording studios are hospitals where musicians go to have their music operated on. I like to get away from that as completely as possible and try to convert the atmosphere and the emotion of the studio into one which is more warm—let's sit around the living room and play music for a while, not even let's sit around the club and play music for a while, which is also a little alien. Music is and always will be a very personal experience.

WILLIAMS: Well, that changes from group to group.

ROTHCHILD: Oh yes, of course, don't misunderstand me, a rock and roll group needs to have an audience to react against; in a recording studio that audience becomes a very specific audience, it's the producer.

He's got to fulfill many functions as an audience. Rather than sitting there and clapping his hands or booing, there are other ways he shows his delight or criticism. What we did, in order to break the cherry of this group in the recording studio, as it were, what I generally like to do is go into the studio first with the musicians feeling that they're going in for a session. *I* realize that we're going to blow a day or two, but we go in to cut masters, we don't go in to screw around. Sometimes you get lucky. We went in and we cut two tunes, neither of which appear on this record. We don't stop at a perfect take, we stop at a take that has the muse in it. That's the most important thing: The take must have the feel, must have the musical feel in it, even if there are musical errors. When the muse comes into the studio to visit us, that's the take.

WILLIAMS: How was it, recording ''The End''?

ROTHCHILD: It was beautiful, it was one of the most beautiful moments I've ever had in a recording studio, that half hour when ''The End'' was recorded. I was emotionally wrung. Usually as a producer you sit there listening for all the things that are right and all the things that are about to go wrong. You're following every instrument simultaneously, you're following the feeling, the mood, all the way through. In this take I was completely, I was absolutely audience. I had done my job, there was nothing actually for me to do once the machines were rolling. I had made sure the sound was right on each instrument, you know, when we did our setup; Bruce [Botnick], the engineer, had been cued by me on everything that I wanted him to do, and at the beginning of the take I was sitting there—producer listening to take.

Midway through I was no longer producer; I was just completely

GLORIA STAVERS

sucked up into it. When we recorded it the studio was totally dark-ened, the only lights visible were a candle burning in the recording studio right next to Jim, whose back was to the control room, singing into his microphone, and the lights on the v.u. meters in the control room. All the other lights were off . . . it was . . . very dark.

WILLIAMS: What studio?

ROTHCHILD: Sunset Sound Recorders, what I feel to be the best studio in the country right now, mainly because of Bruce Botnick, who's twenty-three years old and one of the grooviest engineers I can conceive of, extraordinarily creative and very pleasant to work with. Ah, and Jim . . . it was a magic moment . . . Jim was doing "The End," he was just doing it, for all time, and I was pulled off, right on down his road; he said come with me and I did. It was almost a shock when the song was over, you know when Robby plays those last little tinkling notes on the guitar. It felt like, yeah, you know, like, yes, it's the end, *that's* the end, it cannot go any further, that's the statement.

I felt emotionally washed. There were four other people in the control room at that time, when the take was over and we realized the tape was still going. Bruce, the engineer, was completely sucked along into it and instead of sitting there at attention the way engineers are wont to do, his head was on the console and he was just—immersed. Just absolutely immersed in this take. And he'd done it all, and he'd made all the moves right, because Bruce and I had established a kind of rapport; he knew where I wanted things done and when, and when his work was done he did exactly the same thing, involuntarily, with-out volition; he didn't know he was going to do it, but he became audience, too. So the muse *did* visit the studio that time. And all of us were audience, there was nothing left, the machines knew what to do I guess. It was all right.

WILLIAMS: Jim recorded it on acid?

ROTHCHILD: No, not that one. The night before . . . we tried the night before, we attempted the night before to record "The End," and we couldn't get it. Jim couldn't do it. He wanted desperately to do it, his entire being was screaming, "Kill the father, fuck the mother! Kill the father, fuck the mother!" Now I don't know, have you heard him saying in the middle of "The End" during that big "come" part, have you heard him saying, "kill, kill, kill"?

WILLIAMS: I hear words, I can't tell what they are.

ROTHCHILD: You'll hear it next time. During the whole giant raga thing he's going "kill! kill! kill! kill!" and at another point he's going "fuck, fuck," as a rhythm instrument, the rhythm's going [bangs on microphone] fuck, fuck, fuck, that's down on the track, too, as a rhythm instrument, which is what we intended it to be.

Now, I'm sure that clinically Jim was still on an acid trip; but it was done on the after period, the lucid . . . I guess it isn't that lucid, the clear light period; it's the reflective period of an acid trip. But I have tried several times to record artists on acid and it doesn't work. At least, it doesn't work for me. I have never seen it work in a studio; I have never spoken with a producer who has tried it and has been successful.

WILLIAMS: Maybe the most interesting question is how did "The End" come to be; how much of it had been like that before; and how much of it just suddenly bloomed in those two nights?

ROTHCHILD: Let's put it this way: The frame, the structure of the song was set in everyone's mind, everyone knew what had to be done. Ray knew what he was going to play, not the notes, but where and why it had to be, Robby knew where and why, John—a brilliant drummer, "The End" proved that, in my book that's some of the greatest drumming I've ever heard in my life, irrespective of the fact that I'm involved in this album it's incredibly creative drumming— has an instinct for when. During a very quiet part he'll just come in with three drum shots that are about as loud as you can hit a drum, and they're right, they're absolutely right! Now, you can't plan those things.

Jim, of course, in the recesses of his creative self knew exactly what the song had to be. It went through several permutations in the

GLORIA STAVERS

studio. He'd reach into his back pocket and pull out a sheaf of miscellaneous scraps of paper that had little notes on them, little lines of poetry, and he'd look at them, crumple them up and throw them away, and sing different lines during the tune, lines I'd heard him sing in a club. Other times he'd just riff something I'd never heard before, some of which appears on the record. The version you hear on the record is, I think, a finalized form; it's almost exactly the way they perform it on stage now. It's one of those rare things where a piece of music was caught at the peak of its maturity in a recording studio, extremely rare. The usual situation is that it was recorded too soon or too late; more frequently it was recorded too late. There's a kind of lethargy you hear in a lot of recorded performances that is the result of a piece of music not being caught at its prime, but in its old age. When everybody has their things down pat and there isn't the enthusiasm of creativity.

"Alabama Song," I'm sure you want to know about that. Both Ray and Jim are admirers of Kurt Weill and Bertolt Brecht. For obvious reasons. I guess Brecht was saying in the thirties what Morrison is trying to say in the sixties. They're completely different messages, but both trying to declare a reality to their generation. It's sort of the Doors' tribute to another time, another brave time for some other brave men. And the lyric to "Alabama Song" is strangely contemporary. There is one other verse in the "Alabama Song" which the Doors don't sing, the verse missing is "Show us the way to the next little dollar, oh, don't ask why." And *that* is out of context for the Doors, that's not quite what they had in mind . . .

And, in addition, there is a strange instrument on that tune. It comes from about the nineteen-twenties; it's a variant of the auto-harp. Instead of being strummed or plucked it's struck. The instrument is called a Marxaphone, it was patented under that name. It's a series of steel springs that are located at an angle above the strings; you push down on the steel springs and a little metal hammer at the end goes buoong— It's a percussion instrument, a percussion auto-harp. Ray played it on an overdub. . . . Overdubbing literally means to take your original track and add onto it, putting sound on top of it. Today the system is called sel-synch, it stands for selective synchronization. You can record onto an open track, in synch with the other music.

WILLIAMS: In reference to which, Jim grunts throughout, particularly on "Back Door Man"—his grunts at the beginning are great, just great. And constant noise, throughout "The End" and a lot in "Light My Fire." Does he just have an open mike he can do anything into, you just mix it down because it's on a separate track?

ROTHCHILD: That's right. The lead vocalist is always on a track by himself so that you have absolute flexibility, because listening in a recording studio the perspective's always wrong for making a balanced mix. You're generally listening at very high levels on superb speakers, and unless you can supply everybody in the United States with Altex 605 speakers you're in a world of trouble. So you've got to have absolute flexibility, especially over your lead singer and, if you're lucky, as many other elements as you can in your recording . . . Jim, especially if you see him live, likes to grab the microphone and, uh, he kinda works himself up to a song. He'll grab the microphone and he'll go "uuh," "gaa," "yeaa," and he goes through almost a whole pagan ritual. It's a modern West Coast psychedelic invocation of the muse.

On "End of the Night," Jim decided at the last minute to change the lyric on that. It was originally, and always had been, "take a trip into the end of the night" and at that point Jim decided that the word "trip" had been violently overused, so he changed it to "highway." "End of the Night" is another paean to the, well, it's Jim saying to the world come on, people, get free, get rid of all that shit, take a journey to the great midnight. I'm sure that has meaning for me, and I'm sure that has meaning for you, and I'm sure our meanings are a great deal different. Jim likes to do that.

STRANGE DAYS

All songs written and arranged by the Doors
All lyrics by Jim Morrison except as otherwise noted

STRANGE DAYS

Strange days have found us
Strange days have tracked us down
They're goin' to destroy our
    casual joys
We shall go on playing or find
    a new town

Strange eyes fill strange rooms
Voices will signal their tired end
The hostess is grinning
Her guests sleep from sinning
Hear me talk of sin and you know this
    is it

Strange days have found us
And through their strange hours
We linger alone
Bodies confused
Memories misused
As we run from the day
To a strange night of stone

YOU'RE LOST, LITTLE GIRL

Lyrics by Robby Krieger

You're lost, little girl
You're lost, little girl
You're lost
Tell me who are you

Think that you know what to do
Impossible yes
But it's true

I think that you know what to do
Yeah
Sure that you know what to do

You're lost, little girl
You're lost, little girl
You're lost
Tell me who are you

Think that you know what to do
Impossible yes
But it's true

I think that you know what to do
Girl
Sure that you know what to do

You're lost, little girl
You're lost, little girl
You're lost

LOVE ME TWO TIMES

Lyrics by Robby Krieger

Love me two times, baby
Love me twice today
Love me two times, girl
I'm goin' away

Love me two times, girl
One for tomorrow
One just for today
Love me two times
I'm goin' away

Love me one time
I could not speak
Love me one time
Yeah, my knees got weak

Love me two times, girl
Last me all through the week
Love me two times
I'm goin' away
Love me two times
I'm goin' away

Love me one time
I could not speak
Love me one time
Yeah, my knees got weak

Love me two times, girl
Last me all through the week
Love me two times
I'm goin' away
Love me two times
I'm goin' away

Love me two times, baby
Love me twice today
Love me two times, girl
I'm goin' away

Love me two times, girl
One for tomorrow
One just for today
Love me two times
I'm goin' away

Love me two times, baby
Love me twice today
Love me two times, girl
I'm goin' away

GLORIA STAVERS

GLORIA STAVERS

GLORIA STAVERS

73

UNHAPPY GIRL

Unhappy girl
Left all alone
Playin' solitaire
Playin' warden to your soul
You are locked in a prison of your
    own devise
And you can't believe what it
    does to me
To see you cryin'

Unhappy girl
Tear your web away
Saw thru all your bars
Melt your cell today
You are caught in a prison of your
    own devise

Unhappy girl
Fly fast away
Don't miss your chance
To swim in mystery
You are dying in a prison of your
    own devise

HORSE LATITUDES

When the still sea conspires an armor
And her sullen and aborted
Currents breed tiny monsters
True sailing is dead

Awkward instant
And the first animal is jettisoned
Legs furiously pumping
Their stiff green gallop
And heads bob up
Poise
Delicate
Pause
Consent
In mute nostril agony
Carefully refined
And sealed over

GÜNTER ZINT

MOONLIGHT DRIVE

Let's swim to the moon
Uh-huh
Let's climb thru the tide
Penetrate the evenin' that the city
    sleeps to hide

Let's swim out tonight, love
It's our turn to try
Parked beside the ocean
On our moonlight drive

Let's swim to the moon
Uh-huh
Let's climb thru the tide
Surrender to the waiting worlds that
    lap against our side

Nothin' left open
And no time to decide
We've stepped into a river
On our moonlight drive

Let's swim to the moon
Let's climb thru the tide
You reach a hand to hold me
But I can't be your guide

Easy to love you as I watch you glide
Falling through wet forests
On our moonlight drive
Moonlight drive

C'mon, baby, gonna take a little ride
Goin' down by the ocean side
Gonna get real close
Get real tight
Baby gonna drown tonight
Goin' down, down, down

PEOPLE ARE STRANGE

People are strange when you're
   a stranger
Faces look ugly when you're alone
Women seem wicked when you're
   unwanted
Streets are uneven when you're down

When you're strange
Faces come out of the rain
When you're strange
No one remembers your name

When you're strange
When you're strange
When you're strange

People are strange when you're
   a stranger
Faces look ugly when you're alone
Women seem wicked when you're
   unwanted
Streets are uneven when you're down

When you're strange
Faces come out of the rain
When you're strange
No one remembers your name

When you're strange
When you're strange
When you're strange

MY EYES HAVE SEEN YOU

My eyes have seen you
My eyes have seen you
My eyes have seen you
Stand in your door
Meet inside
Show me some more
Show me some more
Show me some more

My eyes have seen you
My eyes have seen you
My eyes have seen you
Turn and stare
Fix your hair
Move upstairs
Move upstairs
Move upstairs

My eyes have seen you
My eyes have seen you
My eyes have seen you
Free from disguise
Gazing on a city
Under television skies
Television skies
Television skies

My eyes have seen you
My eyes have seen you
My eyes have seen you
Let them photograph your soul
Memorize your alleys
On an endless roll
Endless roll
Endless roll
Endless roll

I CAN'T SEE YOUR FACE

I can't see your face in my mind
I can't see your face in my mind
Carnival dogs consume the lines
Can't see your face in my mind

Don't you cry
Baby
Please don't cry
And don't look at me with your eyes

I can't seem to find the right lie
I can't seem to find the right lie

Insanity's horse adorns the sky
Can't seem to find the right lie

Carnival dogs consume the lines
Can't see your face in my mind

Don't you cry
Baby
Please don't cry
I won't need your picture
Until we say good-bye

PAUL FERRARA

WHEN THE MUSIC'S OVER

When the music's over
When the music's over here
When the music's over
Turn out the lights
Turn out the lights
Turn out the lights

When the music's over
When the music's over
When the music's over
Turn out the lights
Turn out the lights
Turn out the lights

For the music is your special friend
Dance on fire as it intends
Music is your only friend
Until the end
Until the end
Until the end

Cancel my subscription to
    the resurrection
Send my credentials to the house
    of detention
I got some friends inside

The face in the mirror won't stop
The girl in the window won't drop
A feast of friends alive she cried
Waiting for me outside

Before I sink into the big sleep
I want to hear
I want to hear
The scream of the butterfly

Come back, baby
Back into my arms

We're getting tired of hangin' around
Waiting around
With our heads to the ground

I hear a very gentle sound
Very near
Yet very far
Very soft
Yet very clear
Come today
Come today

What have they done to the earth?
What have they done to our fair sister?

Ravaged and plundered
And ripped her
And bit her
Stuck her with knives
In the side of the dawn
And tied her with fences
And dragged her down

I hear a very gentle sound
With your ear down to the ground—
We want the world and we want it,
We want the world and we want it, now
Now? NOW!

Persian night! Babe
See the light! Babe
Save us!
Jesus!
Save us!

So when the music's over
When the music's over, yeah
When the music's over
Turn out the light
Turn out the light

For the music is your special friend
Dance on fire as it intends
Music is your only friend
Until the end
Until the end
Until the end

So when the music's over
When the music's over, yeah
When the music's over
Turn out the light
Turn out the light

PART II

WAITING FOR THE SUN

THE SOFT PARADE

WAITING FOR THE SUN

All songs written and arranged by the Doors
All lyrics by Jim Morrison, except as otherwise noted

DAVID SYGAL

NOT TO TOUCH THE EARTH

Not to touch the earth
Not to see the sun
Nothing left to do but run run run
Let's run
Let's run

House upon the hill
Moon is lying still
Shadows of the trees
Witnessing the wild breeze
Come on, baby, run with me
Let's run

Run with me
Run with me
Run with me
Let's run

The mansion is warm at the top of
    the hill
Rich are the rooms and the
    comforts there
Red are the arms of luxuriant chairs
And you won't know a thing till you
    get inside

Dead President's corpse in the
    driver's car
The engine runs on glue and tar
Come on along, not goin' very far
To the East to meet the Czar

Run with me
Run with me
Run with me
Let's run

Some outlaws live by the side of a lake
The minister's daughter's in love with
    the snake
Who lives in a well by the side of
    the road
Wake up, girl, we're almost home
We should see the gates by morning
We should be inside by evening
Sun, sun, sun
Burn, burn, burn

Soon, soon, soon
Moon, moon, moon
I will get you
Soon
Soon
Soon
I am the Lizard King
I can do anything

DOUGLAS KENT HALL

SUMMER'S ALMOST GONE

Summer's almost gone
Summer's almost gone
Almost gone
Yeah
It's almost gone

Where will we be
When the summer's gone?

Morning found us calmly unaware
Noon burned gold into our hair
At night we swam the laughing sea

When summer's gone
Where will we be?
Where will we be?
Where will we be?

Morning found us calmly unaware
Noon burned gold into our hair
At night we swam the laughing sea

When summer's gone
Where will we be?

Summer's almost gone
Summer's almost gone
We had some good times
But they're gone

The winter's coming on
Summer's almost gone

DOUGLAS KENT HALL

WINTERTIME LOVE

Lyrics by Robby Krieger

Wintertime winds blow cold
   this season
Fallin' in love I'm hopin' to be
Wind is so cold
Is that the reason
Keeping you warm, your hands
   touching me

Come with me
Dance, my dear
Winter's so cold this year
You are so warm
My wintertime love to be

Wintertime winds blue and freezin'
Comin' from northern storms in
   the sea
Love has been lost
Is that the reason
Trying so desperately to be free

Come with me
Dance, my dear
Winter's so cold this year
You are so warm
My wintertime love to be

Come with me
Dance, my dear
Winter's so cold this year
You are so warm
My wintertime love to be

THE UNKNOWN SOLDIER

Wait until the war is over
And we're both a little older

The unknown soldier

Breakfast where the news is read
Television children fed
Unborn, living
Living, dead
Bullet strikes the helmet's head

And it's all over for
    the unknown soldier
It's all over for the unknown soldier

"Company, halt!"

"Present arms!"

Make a grave for the unknown soldier
Nestled in your hollow shoulder

The unknown soldier

Breakfast where the news is read
Television children fed
Unborn, living
Living, dead
Bullet strikes the helmet's head

It's all over
The war is over
It's all over
The war is over
It's all over, baby,
All over!

ELEKTRA RECORDS

SPANISH CARAVAN

Lyrics by Robby Krieger

Carry me
Caravan
Take me away
Take me to Portugal
Take me to Spain
Andalusia
With fields of grain

I have to see you
Again and again
Take me
Spanish caravan
Yes
I know you can

Tradewinds find galleons
Lost in the sea
I know where treasure
Is waiting for me
Silver and gold
In the mountains of Spain

I have to see you
Again and again
Take me
Spanish caravan
Yes
I know you can

MY WILD LOVE

My wild love went riding
She rode all the day
She rode to the devil
And asked him to pay

The devil was wiser
It's time to repent
He asked her to give back
The money she spent

My wild love went riding
She rode to the sea
She gathered together
Some shells for her hair

She rode and she rode on
She rode for a while
Then stopped for an evening
And laid her head down

She rode on to Christmas
She rode to the farm
She rode to Japan
And re-entered a town

By this time the weather
Had changed one degree
She asked for the people
To let her go free

My wild love went riding
She rode for an hour
She rode and she rested
And then she rode on

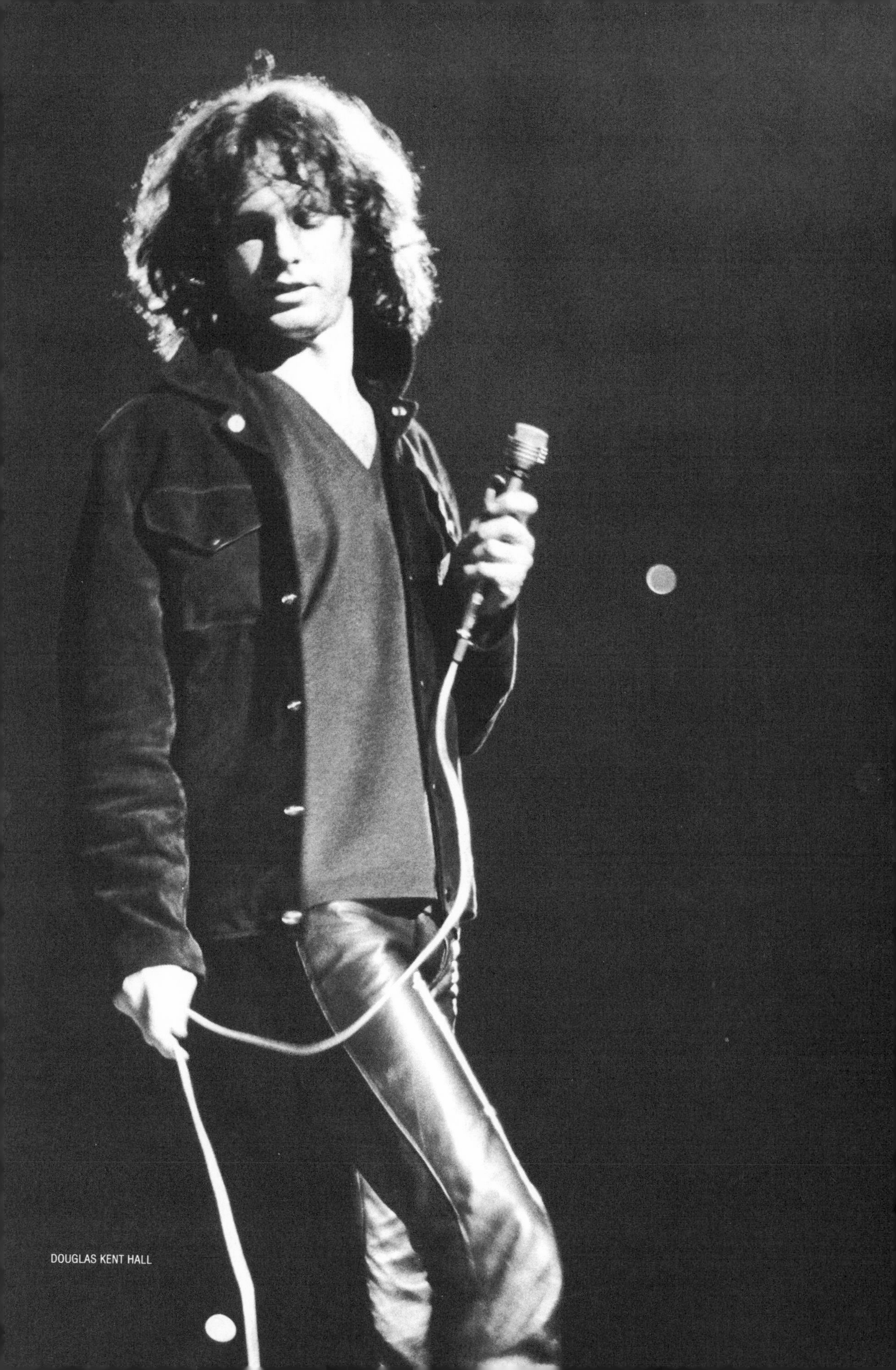

DOUGLAS KENT HALL

WE COULD BE SO GOOD TOGETHER

We could be so good together
Yeah, so good together
We could be so good together
Yeah, we could
I know we could

Tell you lies
I'll tell you wicked lies
Tell you lies
Tell you wicked lies

I'll tell you 'bout the world that
   we'll invent
Wanton world without lament
Enterprise, expedition
Invitation and invention

Yeah
So good together
Ah, so good together
We could be so good together
Yeah, we could
I know we could

We could be so good together
Yeah, so good together
We could be so good together
Yeah, we could
I know we could

Tell you lies
Tell you wicked lies
Tell you lies
Tell you wicked lies

The time you wait subtracts from joy
Beheads these angels you destroy
Angels fight
Angels cry
Angels dance and angels die

We could be so good together
Yeah, so good together
We could be so good together
Yeah, we could
I know we could

YES THE RIVER KNOWS

Lyrics by Robby Krieger

Please believe me
The river told me
Very softly
Want you to hold me

Free fall flow river, flow
On and on it goes
Breathe under water till the end

Free fall flow river, flow
On and on it goes
Breathe under water till the end

Yes the river knows

Please believe me
If you don't need me
I'm going
But I need a little time

I promised I would drown myself
In mystic heated wine

Please believe me
The river told me
Very softly
Want you to hold me

I'm going but I need a little time
I promised I would drown myself
In mystic heated wine

Free fall flow river, flow
On and on it goes
Breathe under water till the end

Free fall flow river, flow
On and on it goes
Breathe under water till the end

FIVE TO ONE

Five to one, baby
One in five
No one here gets out alive
Now
You get yours, baby
I'll get mine
Gonna make it, baby
If we try

The old get old and the young
    get stronger
May take a week and it may
    take longer
They got the guns but we got
    the numbers
Gonna win
Yeah, we're takin' over
Come on

Your ballroom days are over, baby
Night is drawing near
Shadows of the evening crawl across
    the years
You walk across the floor with a
    flower in your hand
Trying to tell me no one understands
Trade in your hours for a handful
    of dimes
Gonna make it, baby
In our prime
Get together one more time

Get together one more time
Get together one more time
Get together one more time
Get together one more time

Well, c'mon, honey
Get along home and wait for me
Baby, I'll be home in just a little while
Y'see, I gotta go out in this car with these people
And get fucked up

Get together one more time
Get together one more time

Get together, gotta get together
Gotta get together, got to
Take you up in the mountains
Ha, ha, ha ha

Love my girl
She's lookin' good
Lookin' real good
C'mon love ya
Feel, hey
Come on

HELLO, I LOVE YOU

Hello, I love you
Won't you tell me your name?
Hello, I love you
Let me jump in your game
Hello, I love you
Won't you tell me your name?
Hello, I love you
Let me jump in your game

She's walkin' down the street
Blind to ev'ry eye she meets
Do you think you'll be the guy
To make the queen of the angels sigh?

Hello, I love you
Won't you tell me your name?
Hello, I love you
Let me jump in your game
Hello, I love you
Won't you tell me your name?
Hello, I love you
Let me jump in your game

She holds her head so high
Like a statue in the sky
Her arms are wicked and her legs
   are long
When she moves my brain screams
   out this song

Sidewalk crouches at her feet
Like a dog that begs for
   something sweet
Do you hope to make her see
   you, fool?
Do you hope to pluck this dusky jewel?
Hello
Hello
Hello
Hello
Hello
Hello
Hello
I want you
I need you

Love
Love
Hello
Hello
Hello

ELLIOT LANDY

LOVE STREET

She lives on Love Street
Lingers long on Love Street
She has a house and garden
I would like to see what happens

She has robes and she has monkeys
Lazy diamond studded flunkies
She has wisdom and knows
    what to do
She has me and she has you

She has wisdom and knows
    what to do
She has me and she has you

I see you live on Love Street
There's the store where the
    creatures meet
I wonder what they do in there
Summer Sunday and a year
I guess I like it fine, so far

She lives on Love Street
Lingers long on Love Street
She has a house and garden
I would like to see what happens

La, la, la, la, la, la
La, la, la, la, la, la
La, la, la, la, la, la
La, la, la, la, la, la
La, la, la, la, la, la

MIKE BARICH

STAGE DOORS

BY HARVEY PERR

This article originally appeared in the L.A. Free Press *in 1969, just following the release of* The Soft Parade, *a time during the Doors' career when they were receiving more than their fair share of negative press. When the issue containing this article arrived at the Doors' office in West Hollywood, it was passed around until everybody had read it. Jim, Robby, Ray, and John enjoyed the piece so much they chose to have it included in their forthcoming songbook.*

The art of the Doors is more and more removed from those standards of art by which rock music is measured. It is, therefore, understandable that the Doors keep getting the worst imaginable reviews from those who put them on some sort of rock pedestal in the first place. It is also understandable that the Doors are still around and are likely to remain around forever, despite all their critics. The trouble is that the Doors have not conformed to fashion and have not, as almost every other major rock group has done, made a fetish of growing, changing, developing, and reverting to form. They have, instead, played out their own fantasies at their own pace in their own way, saying the hell with everything else. The result was a subtler, deeper growth than that of almost all of their contemporaries. But, as I said, it is not as a rock group that these changes have taken place; it has become increasingly clear that their art is the art of restlessness and rebellion, the art of getting through that restlessness and that rebellion by personal investment, by the piling up of obsessive, compulsive images: the art, finally, of poetry and drama, where the personal and the obsessive are the shrines at whose feet true artists always worship.

So, it's a matter of little importance if there has been no real change between "Light My Fire" and "Tell All the People," if their sound has become monotonously familiar, if they have chosen to continue writing variations on a theme rather than creating new themes. Commitment, not versatility, is the key to Art. And in the intensity with which the Doors have made a commitment lies the true measure of their talent, maybe even their genius.

Where the Doors have arrived, in terms of maturity, and of making some new statement about themselves and on their restless art, was there for all to see in their two appearances recently at the Aquarius Theater, where they recorded a live album. This album, I'm sure, will convince everyone that the Doors have gotten it together, because the electricity in the air, the magic that was created that evening, was a testament to the fact that whatever it was the Doors had once upon a time, when they and their world were younger, they not only had again in spades but had the added virtue of being as sublime and self-assured as they were once brash and vulgar (not vulgar in the bad sense, since the best rock-and-roll has always had more than a trace of real vulgarity, which after all is a true American trait, and not necessarily one to be ashamed of or to avoid on artistic terms).

There was Jim Morrison, more the rabbinical student than the Sex God and looking more comfortable in the new guise. Seeming less self-conscious, but singing, if anything, better than even his greatest fans thought he could sing, and projecting truer Sex than he ever did when he writhed calculatedly, because the Sex was warmer, more secure. Not that he wasn't capable of the old theatrical excitement as he proved in one electrifying moment when he disappeared from the stage for a few minutes, then showed up, suddenly in a blue flame (all right, so it was only a blue light shining on him!), above the audience's head (on the scaffold, left over from the *Hair* set), growling out "The Celebration of the Lizard." For me, it was the personal

pleasure of seeing what Morrison could really do, since the only other live appearance of the Doors that I had seen was the Hollywood Bowl concert, which was a drag. It was the excitement of seeing them live up to an image that had become all but distorted, for surely the bum rapping the Doors have received in the past year was as out of proportion to the reality of their talent as perhaps the early praise was. That, indeed, may be the real tragedy of their public image, the fact that they were praised too much too soon and were forced almost immediately, before getting a chance to move on in their own direction, to become a commercial commodity, to have to live up to an already overblown success image.

I am glad that I resisted the first album, convinced at the time that nothing that was so instantly popular could have any real value, because, as a result of my resistance, I didn't get carried away by the hype. I think now that the first album is a fine one, perhaps the finest if an album is to be measured in its totality, but I don't think it is the only one and every single subsequent album has had high points that far surpassed even the best things on the first album. Perhaps the first real attraction to the Doors came with "Waiting for the Sun," because there's something about the underdog (and the harsh reviews of that album suddenly turned the heroes into underdogs) and the vulnerability of the underdog that forces one to consider and appreciate more genuinely where it is he has failed. And it was under this light that it became clear that the Doors hadn't failed at all, except in the eyes of a fickle audience, and that they were pushing toward something that may not have immediately fascinated their public but which was successful on its own terms, successful in defining what the hell the Doors were all about, if indeed they were about anything (and I, for one, think they were and are).

How can we dismiss anyone who gave us "The End" and "When the Music's Over," which have got to be in some sort of pantheon when the rock era is ultimately re-evaluated, and now "The Soft Parade"? How can we fail to see the inner poetry become the dark un-

106

derside of life as "Break on Through" moves to "You're Lost, Little Girl" and finally does make that prophetic breakthrough with the excessively romantic, but always true to the spirit of the Doors (for isn't Revolution as much a form of Romanticism as anything else), "Touch Me"? How can Morrison be accused of singing less well just because the hostility and the sensuality have given way to something richer textured, fuller, more aggressively grim? And when Ray Manzarek's organ playing is ripped apart, isn't it because he has stubbornly insisted on refining his own unique sound (and it is uniquely his, it is part of whatever charisma the Doors have ever had, that whether you think it's bad or good, you always know it's the Doors, and that is Personal and therefore Art) instead of indulging himself in the fancy flourishes of most of his peers? I'm not altogether sure that my own admiration of the Doors has anything to do with their music. Instead it's the impression I get from them because of the thing I feel they're trying to get into and get us into, a world that transcends the limited one of rock, and moves into areas of film and theater and revolution. Seeing Morrison not on stage but living his life, in those quieter moments: seeing him at a production of Norman Mailer's *The Deer Park,* at every performance of the Living Theatre (just prior to, incidentally, the Miami incident), at the opening of the Company Theatre's James Joyce Memorial Liquid Theatre (when he was still a fugitive, taking chances); always in the right place at the right time, involved furiously in the kind of art that is pertinent rather than tangential living. That kind of person doesn't have to have poetry in him but if he does, when he does, you tend to look at it more closely, take it more seriously. In the case of Jim Morrison and the Doors, it is worth the trouble. They have approached Art, no matter how much they have offended, amused, or even thrilled the rock critics. The standards by which art must be measured are older, deeper.

THE SOFT PARADE

All songs written and arranged by the Doors
All lyrics by Jim Morrison, except as otherwise noted

TELL ALL THE PEOPLE

Lyrics by Robby Krieger

Tell all the people that you see
Follow me
Follow me down

Tell all the people that you see
Set them free
Follow me down

You tell them they don't have to run
We're gonna pick up everyone
Come on, take me by the hand
Gonna bury all our troubles in the
    sand
Oh yeah

Can't you see the wonder at your feet
Your life's complete
Follow me down
Can't you see me growing, get your
    guns
The time has come
To follow me down

Follow me across the sea
Where milky babies seem to be molded
    flowing revelry
With the one that set them free

Tell all the people that you see
It's just me
Follow me down

Tell all the people that you see
Follow me
Follow me down

Tell all the people that you see
We'll be free
Follow me down

Tell all the people that you see
It's just me
Follow me down

Tell all the people that you see
Follow me
Follow me down

Follow me down
You got to follow me down
Follow me down

Tell all the people that you see
We'll be free
Follow me down

DOUGLAS KENT HALL

PAUL FERRARA

TOUCH ME

Lyrics by Robby Krieger

C'mon, c'mon, c'mon, c'mon now
Touch me, babe
Can't you see that I am not afraid
What was that promise that you made
Why won't you tell me what she said
What was that promise that she made

Now I'm gonna love you till the heavens
    stop the rain
I'm gonna love you till the stars fall from
    the sky
For you and I

C'mon, c'mon, c'mon, c'mon now
Touch me, baby
Can't you see that I am not afraid
What was that promise that you made
Why won't you tell me what she said
What was that promise that she made

I'm gonna love you till the heavens stop
    the rain
I'm gonna love you till the stars fall from
    the sky
For you and I

I'm gonna love you till the heavens stop
    the rain
I'm gonna love you till the stars fall from
    the sky
For you and I

SHAMAN'S BLUES

There will never be another one
Like you
There will never be another one
   who can
Do the things you do, Oh
Will you give another chance?
Will you try a little try?
Please stop and you'll remember
We were together
Anyway

All right!

Now, if you have a certain evening
You could lend to me
I'd give it all right back to you
Know how it has to be, with you
I know your moods
And your mind
And your mind
And your mind
And your mind
And you're mine

Will you stop to think and wonder
Just what you'll see
Out on the train-yard
Nursing penitentiary

It's gone
I cry
Out long

Did you stop to consider
How it will feel,
Cold grinding grizzly bear jaws
Hot on your heels
Do you often stop and whisper
In Saturday's shore
The whole world's a savior,
Who could ever ever ever ever ever ever
Ask for more?

Do you remember?
Will you stop
Will you stop, the pain?

There will never be another one
Like you
There will never be another one
    who can
Do the things you do, Oh
Will you give another chance?
Will you try a little try?
Please stop and you'll remember
We were together
Anyway

All right

How you must think and wonder
How I must feel
Out on the meadows
While you're on the field

I'm alone for you
And I cry

"He's sweatin', look at him . . .
    optical promise . . .
you'll be dead and in hell before
    I'm born . . .
sure thing . . . bridesmaid . . .
    the only solution . . .
Isn't it amazing?"

DO IT

Ha, ha, ha, ha
Yeah
Please me, yeah
Please, baby
Please, please

Please, please, listen to me children
Please, please, listen to me children
Please, please, listen to me children
Please, please, listen to me children
You are the ones who will rule
    the world

Listen to me children
Listen to me children
Please, please, listen to me children
Please, please, listen to me children
You are the ones who will rule
    the world

You gotta please me
All night

Please, please, listen to me children
Said please, please, listen
    to me children
Please
Yeah, please me
I'm askin' you

Please, please, listen to me children
Please, please, listen to me children
Please, please, listen to me children
Please, my children
Please, children
Please
Children

EASY RIDE

And I know
It will be
An easy ride, all right
And I know
It will be
An easy ride, okay

The mask that you wore
My fingers would explore
The costume of control
Excitement soon unfolds

And I know
It will be
An easy ride, yeah
Joy fought vaguely
With your pride
With your pride

Like polished stone
Like polished stone
I see your eyes
Like burning glass
Like burning glass
I hear you smile
Smile, babe

The mask that you wore
My fingers would explore
The costume of control
Excitement soon unfolds

Easy, baby

Coda queen—be my bride
Rage in darkness by my side
Seize the summer in your pride
Take the winter in your stride
Let's ride

Easy, easy . . .
All right

PAUL FERRARA

WILD CHILD

Wild child
Full of grace
Savior of the human race
Your cool face

Natural child
Terrible child
Not your mother's or your
Father's child
You're our child
Screamin' wild

(An ancient lunatic reigns in the trees
    of the night)

With hunger at her heels
And freedom in her eyes
She dances on her knees
Pirate prince at her side
Staring
Into
The hollow idol's eye

Wild child
Full of grace
Savior of the human race
Your cool face
Your cool face
Your cool face

(You remember when we were
    in Africa?)

RUNNIN' BLUES

Lyrics by Robby Krieger

Poor Otis dead and gone
Left me here to sing his song
Pretty little girl with the red dress on
Poor Otis dead and gone

Back down, turn around slowly
Try it again
Remembering when
It was easy, try it again
Much too easy—remembering when

All right, look at my shoes
Not quite the walkin' blues
Don't fight, too much to lose
Can't fight the runnin' blues

Well, I've got the runnin' blues
Runnin' away, back to L.A.
Got to find the dock on the bay
Maybe find it in L.A.

Runnin' scared, runnin' blue
Goin' so fast, what'll I do?

Well, I've got the runnin' blues
Runnin' away, back to L.A.
Got to find the dock on the bay
Maybe find it back in L.A.

All right, look at my shoes
Not quite the walkin' blues
Don't fight, too much to lose
Can't fight the runnin' blues

All right, look at my shoes
Not quite the walkin' blues
Don't fight, too much to lose
Can't fight the runnin' blues

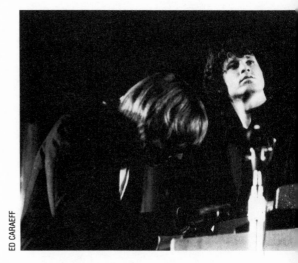

WISHFUL SINFUL

Lyrics by Robby Krieger

Wishful crystal
Water covers everything in blue
Cooling water

Wishful sinful, our love is beautiful
    to see
I know where I would like to be
Right back where I came

Wishful sinful, wicked blue
Water covers you
Wishful, sinful, wicked you
Can't escape the blue

Magic rising
Sun is shining deep beneath the sea
But not enough for you and me
    and sunshine

Love to hear the wind cry

Wishful sinful, our love is beautiful
    to see
I know where I would like to be
Right back where I came

Wishful sinful, wicked blue
Water covers you
Wishful sinful wicked
Can't escape the blue

Love to hear the wind cry
Love to hear cryin'

ED CARAEFF

THE SOFT PARADE

When I was back there in
   seminary school
There was a person there
Who put forth the proposition
That you can petition the Lord
   with prayer
Petition the Lord with prayer
Petition the Lord with prayer
You cannot petition the Lord
   with prayer

Can you give me sanctuary
I must find a place to hide
A place for me to hide
Can you find me soft asylum
I can't make it any more
The man is at the door

Peppermint miniskirts,
   chocolate candy
Champion sax and a girl named Sandy

There's only four ways to get unraveled
One is to sleep and the other is travel

One is a bandit up in the hills
One is to love your neighbor till
His wife gets home

Catacombs, nursery bones
Winter women growing stones
(Carrying babies to the river)

Streets and shoes, avenues
Leather riders selling news

(The monk bought lunch)

Successful hills are here to stay
Everything must be this way
Gentle street where people play
Welcome to the soft parade

All our lives we sweat and save
Building for a shallow grave
Must be something else we say
Somehow to defend this place
(Everything must be this way
Everything must be this way)

The soft parade has now begun
Listen to the engines hum
People out to have some fun
A cobra on my left
Leopard on my right

Deer woman in a silk dress
Girls with beads about their necks
Kiss the hunter of the green vest
Who has wrestled before
With lions in the night

Out of sight

The lights are getting brighter
The radio is moaning
Calling to the dogs
There are still a few animals
Left out in the yard
But it's getting harder
To describe
Sailors
To the underfed

Tropic corridor
Tropic treasure
What got us this far
To this mild Equator
We need someone or something new
Something else to get us through

Calling on the dogs
Calling on the dogs
Calling on the dogs
Calling in the dogs
Calling all the dogs
Calling on the gods

Meet me at the crossroads
Meet me at the edge of town
Outskirts of the city
Just you and I
And the evening sky
You'd better come alone
You'd better bring your gun
We're gonna have some fun

When all else fails
We can whip the horses' eyes
And make them sleep
And cry. . . .

WHO SCARED YOU?

Who scared you, why were you born, my babe
Into time's arms with all of your charms, my love
Why were you born, just to play with me
To freak out or to be beautiful, my dear

Load your head, blow it up, feeling good, baby
Load your head, blow it up, feeling good, baby

Well, my room is so cold, you know you don't have to go, my babe
And if you warm it up right, I'm gonna love you tonight, my love
Well, I'm glad that we came, I hope you're feeling the same
Who scared you and why were you born, please stay

I see a rider coming down the road
Got a burden carrying a heavy load
One sack of silver and one bag of gold

NOTE: This song was recorded during the sessions for *The Soft Parade* but was never included on that album.

PART III

MORRISON HOTEL/ HARD ROCK CAFE

L.A. WOMAN

MORRISON HOTEL/HARD ROCK CAFE

All songs written and arranged by the Doors
All lyrics by Jim Morrison, except as otherwise noted

ROADHOUSE BLUES

Keep your eyes on the road
Your hands upon the wheel
Keep your eyes on the road
Your hands upon the wheel
Yeah, we're goin' to the roadhouse
Gonna have a real good time

Yeah, in back of the roadhouse
They got some bungalows
Yeah, in back of the roadhouse
They got some bungalows
And that's for the people
Who like to go down slow

Let it roll, baby, roll
Let it roll, baby, roll
Let it roll, baby, roll
Let it roll
All night long

Ashen lady
Ashen lady
Give up your vows
Give up your vows

Save our city
Save our city
Right now

Well, I woke up this mornin'
I got myself a beer
Yeah, I woke up this mornin'
I got myself a beer
The future's uncertain
And the end is always near

Let it roll, baby, roll
Let it roll, baby, roll
Let it roll, baby, roll
Let it roll
All night long

WAITING FOR THE SUN

At first flash of Eden we raced down
    to the sea
Standing there on freedom's shore

Waiting for the sun
Waiting for the sun
Waiting for the sun

Can't you feel it, now that spring has
    come
That it's time to live in the scattered
    sun

Waiting for the sun
Waiting for the sun
Waiting for the sun
Waiting for the sun
Waiting . . .

Waiting for you to come along
Waiting for you to hear my song
Waiting for you to come along
Waiting for you to tell me what went wrong

This is the strangest life I've ever
    known

Can't you feel it, now that spring has
    come
That it's time to live in the scattered
    sun

Waiting for the sun
Waiting for the sun
Waiting for the sun
Waiting for the sun

YOU MAKE ME REAL

I really want you
Really do
Really need you, baby
God knows I do
'Cause I'm not real enough
    without you
Oh, what can I do?

You make me real
You make me feel
Like lovers feel

You make me throw away
    mistake and misery
Make me free, love
Make me free

I really want you
Really do
Really need you, baby
Really do
I'm not real enough without you
Oh, what can I do?

You make me real
Only you, baby
Have that appeal

So let me slide in your tender
    sunken sea
Make me free, love
Make me free

Roll now, baby, roll
Well, roll now, baby, roll
You gotta roll now, baby, roll
Roll now, honey, roll
You gotta roll now, baby, roll

Make me free
You make me real
You make me feel
Like lovers feel

You make me throw away
    mistake and misery
Make me free, love
Make me free

Make me free
You make me free

PEACE FROG

There's blood in the streets it's up to
   my ankles
Blood in the streets it's up to my knee
Blood in the streets of the town
   of Chicago
Blood on the rise, it's following me

   She came . . .
   Just about the break of day
   She came, then she drove away
   Sunlight in her hair

Blood on the streets runs a river
   of sadness
Blood in the streets, it's up to my thigh
The river runs down the legs of the city
The women are crying red rivers
   of weeping

   She came in town and then she
     drove away
   Sunlight in her hair

Indians scattered on dawn's
   highway bleeding
Ghosts crowd the young child's fragile
   egg-shell mind

Blood in the streets in the town of
   New Haven
Blood stains the roofs and the palm
   trees of Venice
Blood in my love in the
   terrible summer
Bloody red sun of phantastic L.A.

Blood screams her brain as they chop
   off her fingers
Blood will be born in the birth
   of a nation
Blood is the rose of mysterious union

There's blood in the streets it's up to
   my ankles
Blood in the streets it's up to my knee
Blood in the streets of the town
   of Chicago
Blood on the rise, it's following me

BLUE SUNDAY

I found my own true love
Was on a blue Sunday
She looked at me and told me
I was the only one in the world
Now I have found my girl

My girl awaits for me in tender time
My girl is mine
She is the world
She is my girl

My girl awaits for me in tender time
My girl is mine
She is the world
She is my girl

PAUL FERRARA

SHIP OF FOOLS

The human race was dying out
No one left to scream and shout
People walking on the moon
Smog will get you pretty soon

Ev'ryone was hangin' out
Hangin' up and hangin' down
Hangin' in and holdin' fast
Hope our little world will last

Along came Mister Goodtrips
Looking for a new ship
Come on, people, better climb on board
Come on, baby, now we're going home

Ship of fools
Ship of fools

The human race was dying out
No one left to scream and shout
People walking on the moon
Smog gonna get you pretty soon

Ship of fools
Ship of fools
Ship of fools
Ship of fools
Ship of fools
Ship of fools
Ship of fools

Yeah, climb on board
Ship's gonna leave ya far behind
Climb on board

Ship of fools
Ship of fools

LAND HO!

Grandma loved a sailor who sailed
    the frozen sea
Grandpa was that whaler and he took
    me on his knee
He said "Son, I'm goin' crazy from
    livin' on the land
Got to find my shipmates and walk
    on foreign sands"

This old man was graceful, with silver
    in his smile
He smoked a briar pipe and he walked
    for country miles
Singing songs of shady sisters and
    old time liberty
Songs of love and songs of death and
    songs to set men free

I've got three ships and sixty men
A course for ports unread
I'll stand at mast, let north winds blow
Till half of us are dead

Land ho!

Well, if I get my hands on a dollar bill
Gonna buy a bottle and drink my fill
If I get my hands on a number five
Gonna skin that little girl alive

If I get my hands on a number two
Come back home and marry you
Marry you
Marry you
All right

Yeah, land ho
Yeah, land ho
Well, if I get back home
And I feel all right
You know I'm gonna love you tonight
Love tonight
Love tonight
Yeah, land ho!

THE SPY

I'm a spy in the house of love
I know the dreams that you're
  dreamin' of
I know the words that you long to hear
I know your deepest secret fear

I'm a spy in the house of love
I know the dreams that you're
  dreamin' of
I know the words that you long to hear
I know your deepest secret fear

I know ev'rything
Ev'rything you do
Ev'rywhere you go
Ev'ryone you know

I'm a spy in the house of love
I know the dreams that you're
  dreamin' of
I know the words that you long to hear
I know your deepest secret fear

I know your deepest secret fear
I know your deepest secret fear
I'm a spy
I can see you
What you do
And I know

138

PAUL FERRARA

QUEEN OF THE HIGHWAY

She was a princess
Queen of the highway
Sign on the road said
"Take us to Madre."
No one could save her
Save the blind tiger
He was a monster
Black dressed in leather

She was a princess
Queen of the highway

Now they are wedded
She is a good girl
Naked as children
Out in the meadow
Naked as children
Wild as can be
Soon to have offspring
Start it all over
Start it all over

American boy
American girl
Most beautiful people in the world
Son of a frontier Indian swirl
Dancing thru the midnight whirl-pool
Formless
Hope it can continue a little
    while longer

PAUL FERRARA

140

INDIAN SUMMER

I love you the best
Better than all the rest
I love you the best
Better than all the rest
That I meet in the summer
Indian summer
That I meet in the summer
Indian summer

I love you the best
Better than all the rest

MAGGIE M'GILL

Miss Maggie M'Gill she lived on a hill
Her daddy got drunk and left her
   no will
So she went down down to
   "Tangie Town"
People down there really like
   to get it on

Now, if you're sad and you're
   feelin' blue
Go out and buy a brand new pair
   of shoes
And you go down, down to
   "Tangie Town"
The people down there really like
   to get it on
Get it on

Illegitimate son of a rock and roll star
Illegitimate son of a rock and roll star
Mom met Dad in the back of a
   rock 'n' roll car
Yeah

Well, I'm an old blues man and I think
   that you understand
I've been singing the blues ever since
   the world began

Maggie
Maggie
Maggie M'Gill
Roll on
Roll on
Maggie M'Gill

Maggie
Maggie
Maggie M'Gill
Roll on
Roll on
Maggie M'Gill

WHISKEY, MYSTICS, & MEN

Well, I'll tell you a story
   of whiskey, mystics, and men
And about the believers,
   and how the whole thing began

First there were women and children
   obeying the moon
Then daylight brought wisdom
   and fever and sickness too soon

You can try to remind me
   instead of the other you can
You can help to insure
   that we all insecure our command

If you don't give a listen
   I won't try and tell your new hand
This is it can't you see
   that we all have our end in the band

And if all the teachers and preachers
   of wealth were arraigned
We could see quite a future
   for me in the literal sands

And if all of the people
   could claim to inspect such regret
Well we'd have no forgiveness,
   forgetfulness, faithful remorse

So I tell you, I tell you,
   I tell you we must send away
We must try to find a new answer
   instead of a way

NOTE: This song was recorded during the sessions for *Morrison Hotel* but was never released.

L.A. WOMAN

All songs written and arranged by the Doors.
All lyrics by Jim Morrison, except as otherwise noted

THE CHANGELING

I live uptown
I live down-town
I live all around

I had money
I had none
I had money
I had none
But I never been so broke that I
    couldn't leave town

I'm a changeling
See me change
I'm a changeling
See me change

I'm the air you breathe
Food you eat
Friends you greet
In the swarming street

See me change
See me change

I live uptown
I live down-town
I live all around

I had money, yeah
I had none
I had money, yeah
I had none
But I never been so broke that I
    couldn't leave town

I'm the air you breathe
Food you eat
Friends you greet
In the swarming street

See me change
See me change

I'm leaving town
On the midnight train
Gonna see me change change
    change

Change, change, change
Change, change, change

LOVE HER MADLY

Lyrics by Robby Krieger

Don't you love her madly
Don't you need her badly
Don't you love her ways
Tell me what you say
Don't you love her madly
Want to be her daddy
Don't you love her face
Don't you love her as she's walking
   out the door
Like she did one thousand
   times before
Don't you love her ways
Tell me what you say
Don't you love her as she's walking
   out the door

All your love, all your love
All your love, all your love
All your love is gone
So sing a lonely song
Of a deep blue dream
Seven horses seem
To be on the mark

Yeah, don't you love her
Don't you love her as she's walking
   out the door

All your love, all your love
All your love, all your love
All your love is gone
So sing a lonely song
Of a deep blue dream
Seven horses seem
To be on the mark

Don't you love her madly
Don't you love her madly
Don't you love her madly

BEEN DOWN SO LONG

Well, I been down so god-damn long
That it looks like up to me
Well, I been down so very damn long
That it looks like up to me
Now, why don't one of you people
C'mon and set me free?

I said warden, warden, warden
Won't you break your lock and key
I said warden, warden, warden
Won't you break your lock and key
Hey, come along here, mister
C'mon and let the poor boy be

Baby, baby, baby
Won't you get down on your knees
Baby, baby, baby
Won't you get down on your knees
C'mon little darlin'
C'mon and give your love to me
Oh, yeah

Well, I been down so god-damn long
That it looks like up to me
Well, I been down so very damn long
That it looks like up to me
Now why don't one of you people
C'mon, c'mon, c'mon
And set me free!

CARS HISS BY MY WINDOW

The cars hiss by my window
Like the waves down on the beach
The cars hiss by my window
Like the waves down on the beach
I got this girl beside me
But she's out of reach

Headlights thru my window
Shining on the wall
Headlights thru my window
Shining on the wall
Can't hear my baby
Tho' I call and call

Window started tremblin'
With those sonic booms
Window started to tremble
With those sonic boom, boom
A cold girl'll kill you
In a darkened room

ELEKTRA RECORDS

L.A. WOMAN

Well, I just got into town about
    an hour ago
Took a look around, see which way
    the wind blow
Where the little girls in their
    Hollywood bungalows
Are you a lucky little lady in the
    city of light?
Or just another lost angel

City of night
City of night
City of night
City of night

L.A. woman, L.A. woman
L.A. woman, Sunday afternoon
L.A. woman, Sunday afternoon

L.A. woman, Sunday afternoon
Drive thru your suburbs
Into your blues
Into your blues
Into your blue, blue, blues
Into your blues

I see your hair is burning
Hills are filled with fire
If they say I never loved you
You know they are a liar

Drivin' down your freeway
Midnight alleys roam
Cops in cars, the topless bars
Never saw a woman so alone
So alone, so alone, so alone

Motel money
Murder madness
Let's change the mood
From glad to sadness

Mister Mojo risin'
Mister Mojo risin'
Mister Mojo risin'
Mister Mojo risin'
Got to keep on risin'

JOSEPH SIA

150

Mister Mojo risin'
Mister Mojo risin'
Mojo risin'
Got my Mojo risin'
Mister Mojo risin'
Got to keep on risin'
Risin' risin'
Goin' right in, right in
Goin' right in, right in
Got to right in, right in
Right in, right in

Well, I just got into town about
    an hour ago
Took a look around, see which way
    the wind blow
Where the little girls in their
    Hollywood bungalows
Are you a lucky little lady in the
    city of light?
Or just another lost angel

City of night
City of night
City of night
City of night

L.A. woman, L.A. woman
L.A. woman
You're my woman

A little L.A. woman, L.A. woman
Hey, hey, come on
L.A. woman, come on

L'AMERICA

I took a trip down to L'America
To trade some beads for a pint of gold
I took a trip down to L'America
To trade some beads for a pint of gold

L'America, L'America
L'America, L'America
L'America, L'America

C'mon people, don't you look so down
You know the rainman's comin'
    to town
He'll change your weather
He'll change your luck
Then he'll teach you how to
    find yourself
L'America

Friendly strangers came to town
All the people put them down
But the women loved their ways
Come again some other day
Like the gentle rain
Like the gentle rain that falls

I took a trip down to L'America
To trade some beads for a pint of gold
I took a trip down to L'America
To trade some beads for a pint of gold

L'America, L'America
L'America, L'America
L'America, L'America
L'America

HYACINTH HOUSE

What are they doing in the
    Hyacinth house
What are they doing in the
    Hyacinth house
To please the lions this day?

I need a brand new friend who doesn't
    bother me
I need a brand new friend who doesn't
    trouble me
I need someone
Who doesn't need me

I see the bathroom is clear,
I think that somebody's near
I'm sure that someone is following me
Oh, yeah

Why did you throw the
    Jack-of-Hearts away?
Why did you throw the
    Jack-of-Hearts away?
It was the only card in the deck that I
    had left to play

And I'll say it again
I need a brand new friend
And I'll say it again
I need a brand new friend
And I'll say it again
I need a brand new friend
The end

THE WASP (TEXAS RADIO AND THE BIG BEAT)

I want to tell you about Texas Radio
   and the big beat
It comes out of the Virginia swamps
Cool and slow, with plenty of precision,
   and a back beat
Narrow and hard to master
Some call it heavenly in its brilliance
Others, mean and rueful of the
   Western dream
I love the friends I have gathered
   together on this thin raft
We have constructed pyramids in
   honor of our escaping
This is the land where the
   Pharaoh died

The Negroes in the forest
   brightly feathered
And they are saying
"Forget the night! Live with us in
   forests of azure
Out here on the perimeter, there are
   no stars
Out here we is stoned—immaculate"

Listen to this I'll tell you about
   the heartache,
I'll tell you about the heartache and
   the loss of God
I'll tell you about the hopeless night
The meager food for souls forgot
Tell you about the maiden with
   wrought iron soul

I'll tell you this
No eternal reward can forgive us now
For wasting the dawn

I'll tell you about Texas Radio
   and the big beat
Soft-driven, slow and mad like some
   new language

Now listen to this I'll tell you
    about Texas
I'll tell you about Texas Radio
I'll tell you about the hopeless night
The wanderin' the Western dream
Tell you about the maiden with
    wrought iron soul

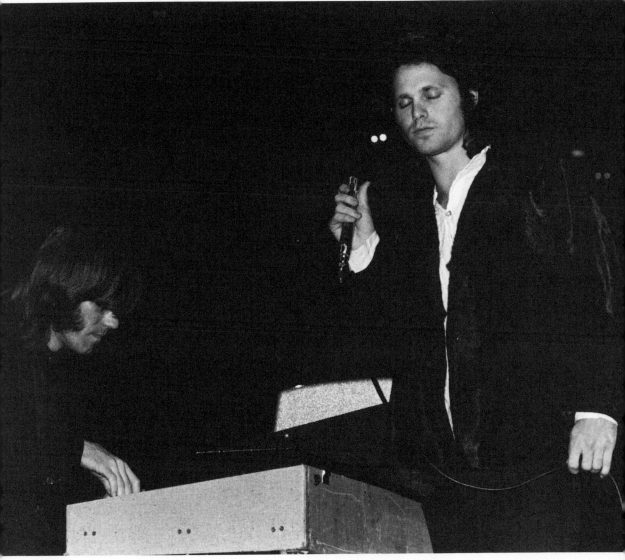

JOSEPH SIA

RIDERS ON THE STORM

Riders on the storm
Riders on the storm
Into this house we're born
Into this world we're thrown
Like a dog without a bone
An actor out on loan
Riders on the storm

There's a killer on the road
His brain is squirming like a toad
Take a long holiday
Let your children play
If you give this man a ride
Sweet family will die
Killer on the road

Girl you gotta love your man
Girl you gotta love your man
Take him by the hand
Make him understand
The world on you depends
Our life will never end
You gotta love your man

Riders on the storm
Riders on the storm
Into this house we're born
Into this world we're thrown
Like a dog without a bone
An actor out on loan
Riders on the storm

Riders on the storm
Riders on the storm
Riders on the storm
Riders on the storm

PARIS BLUES

I wish I was a girl of sixteen
Be the queen of the magazine
I'd drive around in a great big car
I'd have a chauffeur like a movie star
And all night long you could hear me scream!

When you look around, can you believe
   the shape she's in?
When you look all around you, can you believe
   the shape she's in?
Look all around you, can you believe
   the shape she's in?

Know where I'm goin', can't remember
   where I've been
Know right where I'm goin', but I can't remember
   where I've been
Goin' to the city of love, gonna start my life
   all over again

Once I was young now I'm gettin' old
Once I was warm, now I feel cold
Well, I'm goin' overseas, gonna grab me
   some of that gold

NOTE: This song was recorded during the sessions for *L.A. Woman* but was never released.

PART IV

THE DOORS IN CONCERT

AN AMERICAN PRAYER

FOUR DOORS TO THE FUTURE

BY JOHN STICKNEY

For some unknown reason, this obscure article, reprinted from the Williams College News, *in its own brief way comes closer to capturing the Doors live experience than almost any other. Before Miami, before the riots, Pan-ic driven, terrifying, frenetic events, there were the Doors at their ritualistic, hypnotic, majestic best. The word on the street in 1968 regarding the Doors was, "Yeah, their records are great, but you gotta see these guys live." This gives us a good glimpse of why that was.*

"Which one is Jim Morrison?" one girl said to another. But he was not on stage, and a drummer and an organist and a guitar player looked impatiently toward a curtained door.

They sat in darkness punctuated by the steady red lights of amplifiers as tall as a man and the glow of a hundred cigarettes dancing in the evening breeze. The curtain on the door hung like velvet one inch thick.

Two hands pierced the slit of the curtain and drew it back sharply as a spotlight racked the stage and exposed a man who squinted in the brightness. There was applause that he did not care to hear, and the spotlight caught the contempt in the faces of the other musicians as Jim Morrison tentatively fingered the microphone.

He screamed and reeled, throttling the microphone and gazing at a sea of blank faces. He shouted a strung out, distorted and violated stream of word-images which twisted the faces into expressions of shock and yet fascination.

Then there were the drums, crashing against the pulsating rush of the organ while the guitar pirouetted around and through the rhythmic contest with a new sort of terrifying insistence. The Doors were opening as Morrison's words found their way through the circuitous maze of a thousand wires in the impassive deafening amplifiers.

He sang, or rather groaned, or talked to himself out loud as the group raced through "Break on Through" to lead off the set. The band and their instruments work together in complete interaction crystallizing the night air with a texture of sound which a person can run his hand over.

But Morrison gets all the attention, with black curls cascading over the upturned collar of a leather jacket worn the way all leather jackets should be: tight, tough, and somehow menacing. Some people have said that Morrison is beautiful, and others have learned the meaning of the word *charisma* by watching him.

And then there is "Light My Fire," and Morrison's brass and leather voice strokes the lyrics with all the subtlety in which he handles the microphone. The song deserves to be done the Doors' way, with suggestive intonation and instrumentation striving together to produce the incredible erotic pressure of the driving organ-scream climax.

After all, sex is what hard rock is all about. But there is terror in the sexuality of "The End," Morrison's black masterpiece of narrative poetry about a physical and spiritual odyssey which finishes in patricide and incest.

Morrison is at his best in this song, doing his own thing while the organist bends low and presses hard on the keys and the guitarist walks unconcernedly in and out of the spotlight. The drummer sweats.

Morrison dislodged the microphone and staggered blindly across the stage as the lyrics and screams which are "The End" poured out of his mouth, malevolent, satanic, electric and on fire. He stumbled and fell in front of a towering amplifier and sobbed to himself. The guitarist nudged him with the neck of his guitar, and a mouth in the audience said knowingly, "He's stoned."

But he wasn't. He sat up on his knees and stretched out his arms in an attitude of worship toward the cold amplifier, the impartial mediator between the virtues and absurdity of a music dependent upon circuits and ohms.

The audience did not know whether to applaud or not. The guitarist unplugged the electric cord which makes his instrument play, the organist stepped off left, the drummer threw his sticks to the ground in contempt and disgust, and Morrison had disappeared through the velvet curtain without a wave or a smile.

The Doors do not cater to the nameless faces beyond the footlights. The group is not kind, and they do not entertain in any traditional sense. They allow other people to witness the manner of their existence and the pain and pleasure inherent in their imaginations.

The audience was scared, and rightly so. The Doors are not pleasant, amusing hippies proffering a grin and a flower; they wield a knife with a cold and terrifying edge. The Doors are closely akin to the national taste for violence, and the power of their music forces each listener to realize what violence is in himself.

"I think the Doors are a representative American group," says Ray Manzarek, group organist. "America is a melting pot and so are we. Our influences spring from a myriad of sources which we have amalgamated, blending divergent styles into our own thing. We're like the country itself."

Manzarek and Morrison both have degrees from UCLA, and the organist in conversation speaks so articulately and precisely that he gives the impression of being an English professor forced out of academia and into a world of long hair, reverb and the fuzz bass.

The Doors met New York for better or for worse at a press conference in the gloomy vaulted wine cellar of the Delmonico hotel, the perfect room to honor the Gothic rock of the Doors.

It was a good scene. Very few press people, and a lot of the city's rock hangers-on, hirsute and free, were there, all sampling a new sort of high: alcohol. Plastic chicks in mischievous miniskirts sipped daiquiris and waited for Morrison to show. No one was sure he would. But Andy Warhol walked in, and everybody breathed a sigh of relief to find that this indeed was the place to be.

There is a story of the meeting of two electric world-historical heroes; that is, Jim Morrison and Nico, underground film star and singer with Warhol's Velvet Underground. It was love at first sight which later grew into lust, according to a friend of Morrison. Anyway, Warhol seems to be interested in Morrison's potential as a movie star.

Suddenly all eyes turned to the door, where Morrison was making another entrance, sweeping into the room and gathering up the adulation to put in the pocket of his leather jacket.

He put his arm around a reporter, spilling his drink, and compelled him toward the bar. A question which Morrison has been asked before came out somehow, "Jim, were you stoned up there on stage?" And the reply came back. "Man, I'm always stoned."

But apparently Morrison is not into drugs but has stuck with the old American stand-by, alcohol. He got his drink, spoke to the reporter in words which sailed over his head and bounced off the walls of the wine cellar like dead tennis balls. Morrison caromed off and hugged a chick. He was in his element. All eyes were his.

Morrison writes nearly all of the Doors' lyrics, and his work does have meaning. There are rock critics in our time, and when they speak of Morrison's lyrics, visions of Baudelaire, Rimbaud, Joyce and Artaud pop out of their critiques.

But hard rock was never meant for academicism. There is truth in the Doors' beat which drives home the meaning of their fascination with symbolism, streams of consciousness, cruelty and the bizarre in whatever form. That's where the Doors are.

The themes, symbols and imagery of the Doors are stronger in their second album, which manages to transcend the fever-pitch intensity and macabre beauty of their first. The Doors have grown, a good sign.

ELEKTRA RECORDS

THE DOORS IN CONCERT

DOUGLAS KENT HALL

The following compositions originally appeared on the Doors live concert releases Absolutely Live, Alive She Cried, *and* The Doors Live at the Hollywood Bowl. *These titles have recently been deleted from the Doors' recorded catalog of music and have been combined to form one cohesive, definitive concert release, the double CD* The Doors in Concert.

LOVE HIDES

Love hides in the strangest places
Love hides in familiar faces
Love comes when you least expect it
Love hides in narrow corners
Love comes for those who seek it
Love hides inside the rainbow, yeah
Love hides in molecular structures, yeah
Love is the answer

BUILD ME A WOMAN

Give me a witness, darling
I need a witness, babe

I got the poon-tang blues
I got the poon-tang blues
Top of my head down to the bottom of my cowboy shoes alright

Build me a woman, make her ten feet tall
You gotta build me a woman, make her ten feet tall
Don't make her ugly, don't make her . . . oh, small

I'm a Sunday trucker Christian motherfucker
I'm a Sunday trucker Christian motherfucker
I'm a three-eyed boy lookin for a twelve-toed girl

You gotta build me a woman, make her ten feet tall
Build me a woman, make her ten feet tall
Don't make her ugly, don't make her small
Build me someone I can ball all . . . night long

NOTE: Portions of this song were deleted from the recorded version for obvious reasons.

UNIVERSAL MIND

I was doing time in the universal mind
I was feeling fine
I was turning keys, I was setting people free
I was doing alright

Then you came along with a suitcase and a song
Turned my head around
Now I'm so alone, just looking for a home in every face I see
I'm the freedom man, I'm the freedom man
I'm the freedom man, that's how lucky I am

I was doing time in the universal mind
I was feeling fine
I was turning keys, I was setting people free
I was doing alright

Then you came along with a suitcase and a song
Turned my head around
Now I'm so alone, just looking for a home in every face I see
I'm the freedom man

I was doing time in the universal mind
I was feeling fine
I was turning keys, I was setting people free
I was doing alright

Then you came along with a suitcase and a song
Turned my head around
Now I'm so alone, just looking for a home in every face I see
I'm the freedom man, yeah, that's how lucky I am
I'm the freedom man, I'm the freedom man

ANDREW KENT

BREAK ON THROUGH #2
(DEAD CATS, DEAD RATS)

When I was back there in seminary school
There was a person there who put forth the proposition
That you can petition the Lord with prayer
Petition the Lord with prayer
Petition the Lord with prayer
You cannot petition the Lord with prayer

Dead cats, dead rats, did you see what they were at, alright
Dead cat in a top hat

Sucking on a young man's blood
Wishing he could come, yeah
Sucking on the soldier's brain
Wishing it would be the same

Dead cat, dead rat, did you see what they were at
Fat cat in a top hat
Thinks he's an aristocrat
Thinks he can kill and slaughter
Thinks he can shoot my daughter

Dead cats, dead rats, think you're an aristocrat
Crap . . . ha, that's crap

You know the day destroys the night
Night divides the day
Tried to run, tried to hide
Break on through to the other side
Break on through to the other side
Break on through to the other side

Chased our pleasures here
Dug our treasures there
Can you still recall the time we cried
Break on through to the other side
Break on through to the other side
Break on through

Everybody loves my baby
Everybody loves my baby
She gets high
She gets high
She gets high

I found an island in your arms
Country in your eyes
Arms that chained us, eyes that lied
Break on through to the other side
Break on through to the other side
Break on through, yeah . . . alright

Yeah, made the scene week to week
Day to day, hour to hour
Gate is straight, deep and wide
Break on through to the other side
Break on through to the other side

Break on through, break on through
Break on through, break on through

THE CELEBRATION OF THE LIZARD

LIONS IN THE STREET

Lions in the street and roaming
Dogs in heat, rabid, foaming
A beast caged in the heart of the city

The body of his mother rotting in the summer ground
He fled the town
Went down South and crossed the border
Left the chaos and disorder
Back there over his shoulder

One morning he awoke in a green hotel
With a strange creature groaning beside him
Sweat oozed from its shiny skin

Is everybody in?
The ceremony is about to begin!

WAKE UP

Wake up!
You can't remember where it was
Had this dream stopped?

The snake was pale gold, glazed and shrunken
We were afraid to touch it
The sheets were hot dead prisons

And she was beside me, old she's known, young
Her dark red hair, the white soft skin

Now, run to the mirror in the bathroom
Look! She's coming in here
I can't live through each slow century of her moving
I let my cheek slide down the cool smooth tile
Feel the good cold stinging blood
The smooth hissing snakes of rain

172

A LITTLE GAME

Once I had a little game
I liked to crawl back in my brain
I think you know the game I mean
I mean the game called "Go insane"

Now you should try this little game
Just close your eyes, forget your name
Forget the world, forget the people
And we'll erect a different steeple

This little game is fun to do
Just close your eyes, no way to lose
And I'm right here, I'm going too
Release control, we're breaking through

THE HILL DWELLERS

Way back deep into the brain
Way back past the realm of pain
Back where there's never any rain

And the rain falls gently on the town
And over the heads of all of us

And in the labyrinth of streams beneath the
Quiet unearthly presence of
Nervous hill dwellers in the gentle hills around
Reptiles abounding
Fossils, caves, cool air heights

Each house repeats a mold
Windows rolled
A beast car locked in against morning
All now sleeping
Rugs silent, mirrors vacant
Dust blind under the beds of lawful couples
Wound in sheets
And daughters, smug with semen
Eyes in their nipples

Wait! There's been a slaughter here

Don't stop to speak or look around
Your gloves and fan are on the ground

We're getting out of town
We're going on the run
And you're the one I want to come!

NOT TO TOUCH THE EARTH

Not to touch the earth, not to see the sun
Nothing left to do but run, run, run
Let's run, let's run

House upon the hill, moon is lying still
Shadows of the trees witnessing the wild breeze
Come on, baby, run with me
Let's run

Run with me, run with me, run with me
Let's run

The mansion is warm at the top of the hill
Rich are the rooms and the comforts there
Red are the arms of luxuriant chairs
And you won't know a thing till you get inside

Dead president's corpse in the driver's car
The engine runs on glue and tar
Come on along, not going very far
To the east to meet the Czar

Run with me, run with me, run with me
Let's run

Some outlaws live by the side of a lake
The minister's daughter's in love with the snake
Who lives in a well by the side of the road
Wake up, girl! We're almost home, yeah

Sun, sun, sun
Burn, burn, burn
Moon, moon, moon
I will get you soon . . . soon . . . soon!

I am the Lizard King
I can do everything

NAMES OF THE KINGDOM

We came down the rivers and highways
We came down from forests and falls
We came down from Carson and Springfield
We came down from Phoenix enthralled

And I can tell you the names of the kingdom
I can tell you the things that you know
Listening for a fistful of silence
Climbing valleys into the shade

THE PALACE OF EXILE

For seven years I dwelt in the loose palace of exile
Playing strange games with the girls of the island
Now I have come again to the land of the fair
And the strong and the wise

Brothers and sisters of the pale forest
Children of night
Who among you will run with the hunt?

Now night arrives with her purple legion
Retire now to your tents and to your dreams
Tomorrow we enter the town of my birth
I want to be ready

ED CARAEFF

GLORIA

Original version by Van Morrison
Arrangement and new lyrics by the Doors

Tell ya 'bout my baby
She come around
She come 'round here
The head to the ground

Come 'round here
A-just about midnight
She make me feel so good
Make me feel alright

She come 'round my street now
She come to my house, yeah
Knock upon my door
Climbing up my stairs
One two three
Come on up, baby
Mmmm, here she is in my room . . . oh boy!

Hey, what's your name?
How old are you?
Where d'you go to school?

Well, now that we know each other a little
bit better, why don't you come over here?

Make me feel alright!

Gloria
Gloria
Gloria
Gloria
Gloria
All night! All day!
All right! Okay, yeah!

You were my queen and I was your fool
Riding home after school

You took me home, yeah
To your house
Your father's at work
Your mama's out shopping around
Took me into your room
Showed me your thing
Why d'you do it, babe?

A-getting softer, slow it down
Softer, get it down
Now you show me your thing . . . yeah

Wrap your legs around my neck
Wrap your arms around my feet
Wrap your hair around my skin
Wrap your lips around my cock

I'm gonna . . .
It's getting harder
It's getting too darn fast
It's getting harder
Alright! Come on, darling, let's get it on . . .

Whoa, too late! Too late! Too late
Too late! Too late! Too late
It's . . . Stop! . . . Oh

Make me feel alright, babe

G-L-O-R-I-A
G-L-O-R-I-A

Gloria

All night
All day
All right
Okay

Keep the whole thing going, babe!
All right
All right
Fuck
Aaaaaaaaaaaaaaaaaahuh!

NOTE: Portions of this song were deleted from the recorded
version for obvious reasons.

LIGHT MY FIRE
(Including GRAVEYARD POEM)

Lyrics by Robby Krieger
"Graveyard Poem" by Jim Morrison

You know that it would be untrue
You know that I would be a liar
If I was to say to you
Girl, we couldn't get much higher

Come on, baby, light my fire
Come on, baby, light my fire
Try to set the night on fire

Time to hesitate is through
No time to wallow in the mire
Try now, we can only lose
And our love become a funeral pyre

Come on, baby, light my fire
Come on, baby, light my fire
Try to set the night on fire

It was the greatest night of my life
although I still had not found a wife
I had my friends right there beside me
We were close together

We tripped the wall
We scaled the graveyard
Ancient shapes were all around us
The wet dew felt fresh beside the fog
Two made love in an ancient spot
One chased a rabbit into the dark
A girl got drunk and balled the dead
And I gave empty sermons to my head
Cemetery, cool and quiet
Hate to leave your sacred lay
Dread the milky coming of the day

Time to hesitate is through
No time to wallow in the mire
Try now, we can only lose
And our love become a funeral pyre

Come on, baby, light my fire
Come on, baby, light my fire
Try to set the night on fire

Know that it would be untrue
You know that I would be a liar
If I was to say to you
Girl, we couldn't get much higher

Come on, baby, light my fire
Come on, baby, light my fire
Try to set the night on fire
Try to set the night on fire
Try to set the night on fire
Try to set the night on fire

Alright! Alright! Alright!

ED CARAEFF

TEXAS RADIO AND
THE BIG BEAT #2

[Spoken Intro]

I wanna tell you about Texas Radio and the Big Beat
Comes out of the Virginia swamps, cool and slow
With a back beat, narrow and hard to master
Some call it heavenly in its brilliance
Others mean and rueful of the Western dream
I love the friends I have gathered together on this thin raft
We have constructed pyramids in honor of our escaping
Well, this is the land where the Pharaoh died

Children
The river contains specimens
The voices of singing women call us on the far shore
And they are saying:
Forget the night
Live with us in forests of azure

Meager food for souls forgot

I'll tell you this . . .
No eternal reward will forgive us now
For wasting the dawn

And one morning you awoke
And the strange sun
And opening your door . . .

180

THE END

Come on, turn the lights out, man
Turn it way down
Hey Mister Lightman
You gotta turn those lights way down, man!
Hey, I'm not kidding, you gotta turn the lights out
Come on!
What do we care . . . ?

This is the end, beautiful friend
This is the end, my only friend, the end
Of our elaborate plans, the end
Of everything that stands, the end
No safety or surprise, the end
I'll never look into your eyes again

Can you picture what will be
So limitless and free
Desperately in need of some stranger's hand
In a desperate land
Come on, baby!

And we were in this house and there was a sound like
    silverware being dropped on linoleum, and then
    somebody ran into the room and they said
"Have you seen the accident outside?"
And everybody said:
"Hey man, have you seen the accident outside?"

Have you seen the accident outside
Seven people took a ride
Six bachelors and their bride
Seven people took a ride
Seven people died

Don't let me die in an automobile
I wanna lie in an open field
Want the snakes to suck my skin
Want the worms to be my friends
Want the birds to eat my eyes
As here I lie
The clouds fly by

Ode to a grasshopper . . .
I think I'll open a little shop,
A little place where they sell things
And I think I'll call it "Grasshopper" . . .

I have a big green grasshopper out there
Have you seen my grasshopper, mama?
Looking real good . . .

(Oh, I blew it, it's a moth)
That's alright, he ain't got long to go,
   so we'll forgive him

Ensenada
The dog crucifix
The dead seal
Ghosts of the dead car sun
Stop the car
I'm getting out, I can't take it
Hey, look out, there's somebody coming
And there's nothing you can do about it . . .

The killer awoke before dawn
He put his boots on
He took a face from the ancient gallery
And he . . . he walked on down the hallway, baby
Came to a door
He looked inside

Father?
Yes, son?
I wanna kill you
Mother . . . I want to . . .
Fuck you, mama, all night long"
Beware, mama
Gonna love you, baby, all night

Come on, baby, take a chance with us
Come on, baby, take a chance with us
Come on, baby, take a chance with us
Meet me at the back of the blue bus
Meet me at the back of the blue bus,
Blue rock,
Blue bus,
Blue rock
Blue bus

Kill! Kill!

This is the end, beautiful friend
This is the end, my only friend, the end
Hurts to set you free
But you'll never follow me
The end of laughter and soft lies
The end of nights we tried to die
This is the end

SOMEDAY SOON

Someday soon, someday soon
Familiar freaks will fill your living room
Rugs lash out with their lizard tongues, you're not getting young
You're not getting young

And I hate to remind you
   but you're going to die
And you're going to be needing
   all of your eyes

   You'll be all alone
   when the animals cry
   All by yourself
   in the infancy's lie

Someday soon, someday soon
Television bleeding like a harvest moon
Flush the scissors down the hole, you're getting old
You're getting old

And I hate to remind you
   but you're going to die
And you're going to be needing
   all of your lies

   You'll be all alone
   when the animals cry
   All by yourself
   in some infancy's lie

Someday soon, someday soon
Someday soon, someday soon

NOTE: This song was recorded live but never released.

AN AMERICAN PRAYER

ANDREW KENT

An American Prayer *stands as one of the most unique and original LP's of all time. In 1976, five years after the death of Jim Morrison, Robby Krieger remembered some of the poetry Jim had recorded on his twenty-seventh birthday shortly before his departure to Paris. Certain lines and phrases wouldn't leave Krieger alone. Finally, he placed a call to the engineer who had recorded Jim's readings. This auspicious beginning eventually led to Ray Manzarek, John Densmore, and Robby Krieger re-forming to once again set music to the poetry of Jim Morrison in order to give him the poetry album he did not live to complete. It was the last time this combination would work together.*

Jim Morrison was a poet who wrote lyrics and as such never wrote a line that was not directly personal. With the Doors as his vehicle and contemporary music as his medium, his poetry was seen as lyrics and the poet was seen as a star. This record is the mythic rock star shedding that role and talking in a poet's tongue. Once again his words are supported by the Doors' alternately sympathetic and strong music. There are back-glances, interpretations, and insights sprinkled throughout the recording.

We hear Morrison in all his roles: the singer, the performer, the poet, and the person behind the myth. In no way does the album either propel or dispel the Morrison mythology. It does remind us, however, there is more to Jim Morrison (and the Doors) than legend, but also the legend has its foundation in fact. Sometimes the contents of this unique album are in sharp conflict with the myth . . . sometimes indistinguishable from it. Such was the man.

When this album is listened to, it is difficult to believe Jim has left us at all. Essentially An American Prayer *is Jim Morrison by Jim Morrison. Interpreted and made possible by those who knew, loved, and worked intimately with the man.*

When the last segment ends and the record is over, you feel the way you felt when a Doors concert ended . . . a sense of suspension and the eerie feeling you've just experienced something very personal and something very, very special.

1
AWAKE GHOST SONG

Is everybody in?

       Is everybody in?

              Is everybody in?

                     The ceremony is about to begin

                     WAKE UP

Awake

                     You can't remember where it was
                     Had this dream stopped?

Shake dreams from your hair
My pretty child, my sweet one.
Choose the day and choose the sign of your day
The day's divinity
First thing you see

A vast radiant beach in a cool jeweled moon
Couples naked race down by its quiet side
And we laugh like soft, mad children
Smug in the wooly cotton brains of infancy
The music and voices are all around us
Choose, they croon, the Ancient Ones
The time has come again
Choose now, they croon
Beneath the moon
Beside an ancient lake
Enter again the sweet forest
Enter the hot dream
Come with us
Everything is broken up and dances

DAWN'S HIGHWAY

Indians scattered on dawn's highway bleeding
Ghosts crowd the young child's fragile eggshell mind.

Me and my—ah—mother and father—and a
grandmother and a grandfather—were driving through
the desert, at dawn, and a truck load of Indian
workers had either hit another car, or just—I don't
know what happened—but there were Indians scattered
all over the highway, bleeding to death.

So the car pulls up and stops. That was the first time
I tasted fear. I musta' been about four—like a child is
like a flower, his head is just floating in the
breeze, man.

The reaction I get now thinking about it, looking
back—is that the souls of the ghosts of those dead
Indians . . . maybe one or two of 'em . . . were just
running around freaking out, and just leaped into my
soul. And they're still in there.

Indians scattered on dawn's highway bleeding
Ghosts crowd the young child's fragile eggshell mind.

Blood in the streets in the town of New Haven
Blood stains the roofs and the palm trees of Venice
Blood in my love in the terrible summer
Bloody red sun of Phantastic L.A.

Blood screams her brain as they chop off her fingers
Blood will be born in the birth of a nation
Blood is the rose of mysterious union
Blood on the rise, it's following me

Indian, Indian what did you die for?
Indian says, nothing at all.

NEWBORN AWAKENING

Gently they stir, gently rise
The dead are newborn awakening
With ravaged limbs and wet souls
Gently they sigh in rapt funeral amazement
Who called these dead to dance?
Was it the young woman learning to play the ghost song on her baby grand?
Was it the wilderness children?
Was it the ghost god himself, stuttering, cheering, chatting blindly?
I called you up to anoint the earth
I called you to announce sadness falling like burned skin
I called you to wish you well
To glory in self like a new monster
And now I call on you to pray

2
TO COME OF AGE

A military station in the desert

Can we resolve the past
Lurking jaws, joints of time?
The Base
To come of age in a dry place
Holes and caves

My friend drove an hour each day from the mountains
The bus gives you a hard-on with books in your lap
Someone shot the bird in the afternoon dance show
They gave out free records to the best couple
Spades dance best, from the hip

BLACK POLISHED CHROME
LATINO CHROME

The music was new
   black polished chrome
And came over the summer
   like liquid night
The DJ's took pills to stay awake
   and play for seven days
They went to the studio
   And someone knew him
Someone knew the TV showman
He came to our homeroom party
   and played records
And when he left in the hot noon sun
   and walked to his car
We saw the chooks had written
   F-U-C-K on his windshield
He wiped it off with a white rag
   and smiling coolly drove away
He's rich. Got a big car

My gang will get you
Scenes of rape in the arroyo
Seductions in cars, abandoned buildings
Fights at the food stand
The dust

The shoes
Open shirts and raised collars
Bright sculptured hair

Hey man, you want girls, pills, grass? C'mon . . .
I show you good time.
This place has everything. C'mon . . .
I show you.

ANGELS AND SAILORS

Angels and sailors
        rich girls
                backyard fences
                    tents
Dreams watching each other narrowly
          Soft luxuriant cars
Girls in garages, stripped
            out to get liquor and clothes
            half gallons of wine and six-packs of beer
Jumped, humped, born to suffer
            made to undress in the wilderness

        I will never treat you mean
        Never start no kind of scene
        I'll tell you every place and person that I've been

Always a playground instructor, never a killer
Always a bridesmaid on the verge of fame or over
He maneuvered two girls into his hotel room
One a friend, the other, the young one, a newer stranger
Vaguely Mexican or Puerto Rican
Poor boys thighs and buttocks scarred by a father's belt
She's trying to rise
Story of her boyfriend, of teenage stoned death games
Handsome lad, dead in a car
Confusion
No connections
Come 'ere
I love you
Peace on earth
Will you die for me?
Eat me
This way
The end

I'll always be true
Never go out, sneaking out on you, babe
If you'll only show me Far Arden again

I'm surprised you could get it up
He whips her lightly, sardonically, with belt
Haven't I been through enough? she asks
Now dressed and leaving
The Spanish girl begins to bleed
She says her period
It's Catholic heaven
I have an ancient Indian crucifix around my neck
My chest is hard and brown
Lying on stained, wretched sheets with a bleeding virgin
We could plan a murder
Or start a religion

STONED IMMACULATE

I'll tell you this . . .
No eternal reward will forgive us now
For wasting the dawn

Back in those days everything was simpler and more confused
One summer night, going to the pier
I ran into two young girls
The blonde was called Freedom
The dark one, Enterprise
We talked and they told me this story
Now listen to this . . .
I'll tell you about Texas radio and the big beat
Soft driven, slow and mad
Like some new language
Reaching your head with the cold, sudden fury of a divine messenger
Let me tell you about heartache and the loss of god
Wandering, wandering in hopeless night
Out here in the perimeter there are no stars

Out here we is stoned
Immaculate

3
THE MOVIE

The movie will begin in five moments
The mindless voice announced
All those unseated will await the next show

We filed slowly, languidly into the hall
The auditorium was vast and silent
As we seated and were darkened, the voice continued

The program for this evening is not new
You've seen this entertainment through and through
You've seen your birth, your life and death
You might recall all of the rest
Did you have a good world when you died?
Enough to base a movie on?

I'm getting out of here!

Where are you going?

To the other side of morning

Please don't chase the clouds, pagodas

Her cunt gripped him like a warm, friendly hand

It's all right, all your friends are here

When can I meet them?

After you've eaten

I'm not hungry

Uh, we meant beaten

Silver stream, silvery scream
Oooooh, impossible concentration

CURSES, INVOCATIONS

Curses, Invocations
Weird bate-headed mongrels
I keep expecting one of you to rise
Large buxom obese queens
Garden hogs and cunt veterans
Quaint cabbage saints
Shit hoarders and individualists
Drag strip officials
Tight lipped losers and
Lustful fuck salesmen
My militant dandies

All strange order of monsters
Hot on the trail of the woodvine
We welcome you to our procession

Here come the Comedians
Look at them smile
Watch them dance an Indian mile
Look at them gesture
How aplomb
So to gesture everyone
Words dissemble
Words be quick
Words resemble walking sticks
Plant them they will grow
Watch them waver so
   I'll always be a word man
   Better than a bird man

4

AMERICAN NIGHT

All hail the American night!

What was that?
I don't know
Sounds like guns . . . thunder

ROADHOUSE BLUES

Ladies and gentlemen!
From Los Angeles, California . . . The Doors!

A-keep your eyes on the road, your hand upon the wheel
A-keep your eyes on the road, your hand upon the wheel
Come to the road house, gonna have a real a-good time

Yeah, at the back of the road house they got some bungalows
Ah, at the back of the road house they got some bungalows
That's for the people . . . like to go down slow

Let it roll, baby, roll. Let it roll, baby, roll
Let it roll, baby, roll. Let it roll . . . all night long

You gotta roll, roll, roll, gotta thrill my soul, alright
Roll, roll, roll, gotta thrill my soul, you gotta (. . .)
Alright

Ashen Lady, Ashen Lady
Give up your vows, give up your vows
Save our city! Save our city! A-right now!

Well, I woke up this morning, got myself a beer
Well, I woke up this morning, I got myself a beer
Yeah, the future's uncertain, the end is always near

Let it roll, baby, roll. Let it roll, baby roll
Let it roll, baby roll. Let it roll . . . all night long

Alright! Alright! Alright!
Hey, listen! Listen! Listen, man! Listen, man!
I don't know how many you people believe in astrology . . .

Yeah, that's right . . . that's right, baby, I . . . I am a
Sagittarius
The most philosophical of all the signs
But anyway, I don't believe in it
I think it's a bunch of bullshit, myself
But I tell you this, man, I tell you this
I don't know what's gonna happen, man, but I wanna have
my kicks before the whole shithouse goes up in flames
Alright

THE WORLD ON FIRE

The World on Fire . . . Taxi from Africa . . . The Grand Hotel . . .
He was drunk   a big party last night   back, going back
in all directions   sleeping these insane hours   I'll never wake up
in a good mood again   I'm sick of these stinky boots

LAMENT

Lament for my cock
Sore and crucified
I seek to know you
Acquiring soulful wisdom
You can open walls of mystery
Stripshow

How to acquire death in the morning show
TV death which the child absorbs

Deathwell mystery which makes me write
Slow train, the death of my cock gives life

Forgive the poor old people who gave us entry
Taught us god in the child's prayer in the night

Guitar player
Ancient wise satyr
Sing your ode to my cock

Caress its lament
Stiffen and guide us, we frozen
Lost cells
The knowledge of cancer
To speak to the heart
And give the great gift
Words   Power   Trance

This stable friend and the beasts of his zoo
Wild haired chicks
Women flowering in their summit
Monsters of skin
Each color connects
        to create the boat
                which rocks the race
Could any hell be more horrible
                than now
                        and real?

I pressed her thigh and death smiled

Death, old friend
Death and my cock are the world
I can forgive my injuries in the name of
Wisdom   Luxury   Romance

Sentence upon sentence
Words are healing lament
For the death of my cock's spirit
Has no meaning in the soft fire
Words got me the wound and will get me well
If you believe it

All join now and lament for the death of my cock
A tongue of knowledge in the feathered night
Boys get crazy in the head and suffer
I sacrifice my cock on the altar of silence

THE HITCHHIKER

Thoughts in time and out of season
   The Hitchhiker
Stood by the side of the road
And leveled his thumb
In the calm calculus of reason

Hi. How you doin'? I just got back into town L.A.
I was out on the desert for awhile
   Riders on the storm
Yeah. In the middle of it
Riders on the storm
Right . . .
   Into this world we're born
Hey, listen, man, I really got a problem
   Into this world we're thrown
When I was out on the desert, ya know
   Like a dog without a bone
   An actor out on loan
I don't know how to tell you
   Riders on the storm
but, ah, I killed somebody
   There's a killer on the road
No . . .
   His brain is squirming like a toad
It's no big deal, ya know
I don't think anybody will find out about it, but . . .
   Take a long holiday
just, ah . . .
   Let your children play
this guy gave me a ride, and ah . . .
   If you give this man a ride
started giving me a lot of trouble
   Sweet family will die
and I just couldn't take it, ya know?
   Killer on the road
And I wasted him
   Yeah

5

AN AMERICAN PRAYER

Do you know the warm progress
*   under the stars?*
Do you know we exist?
Have you forgotten the keys
*   to the Kingdom*
Have you been borne yet
*   and are you alive?*
Let's reinvent the gods, all the myths
*   of the ages*
Celebrate symbols from deep elder forests
[Have you forgotten the lessons
*   of the ancient war]*
We need great golden copulations
The fathers are cackling in trees
*   of the forest*
Our mother is dead in the sea
Do you know we are being led to
*   slaughters by placid admirals*
And that fat slow generals are getting
*   obscene on young blood*
Do you know we are ruled by TV
The moon is a dry blood beast
Guerrilla bands are rolling numbers
*   in the next block of green vine*
amassing for warfare on innocent
*   herdsmen who are just dying*
O great creator of being
grant us one more hour to
*   perform our art*
*   and perfect our lives*
The moths and atheists are doubly divine
*   and dying*
We live, we die
and death not ends it
Journey we more into the
*   Nightmare*
Cling to life
*   Our passion'd flower*
Cling to cunts and cocks
*   of despair*
We got our final vision
*   by clap*

EDMUND TESKE

196

Columbus' groin got
 filled with green death
(I touched her thigh
 and death smiled)
We have assembled inside this ancient
 and insane theatre
To propagate our lust for life
 and flee the swarming wisdom
 of the streets
The barns are stormed
The windows kept
And only one of all the rest
To dance and save us
With the divine mockery
 of words
Music inflames temperament
(When the true King's murderers
are allowed to roam free
a thousand Magicians arise
 in the land)
Where are the feasts
we were promised
Where is the wine
The New Wine
 (dying on the vine)
resident mockery
give us an hour for magic
We of the purple glove
We of the starling flight
 and velvet hour
We of arabic pleasure's breed
We of sundome and the night
Give us a creed
To believe
A night of Lust
Give us trust in
The Night
Give of color
Hundred hues
a rich mandala
For me and you
And for your silky
pillowed house

A head, wisdom
And a bed
Troubled decree

Resident mockery
has claimed thee
We used to believe
In the good old days
We still receive
In little ways
The Things of Kindness
An unsporting brow
Forget and allow
Did you know freedom exists
  in a school book
Did you know madmen are
  roaming our prison
within a jail, within a gaol
within a white free protestant
maelstrom
We're perched headlong
  on the edge of boredom
We're reaching for death
  on the end of a candle
We're trying for something
  That's already found us

We can invent Kingdoms of our own
grand purple thrones, those chairs of lust
and love we must, in beds or rust
Steel doors lock in prisoner's screams
and muzak, AM, rocks their dreams
No black men's pride to hoist the beams
while mocking angels sift what seems
To be a collage of magazine dust
Scratched on foreheads of walls of trust
This is just jail for those who must
get up in the morning and fight for such
unusable standards
while weeping maidens
show-off penury and pout
ravings for a mad
*staff**

Wow, I'm sick of doubt
Live in the light of certain
South
Cruel bindings
The servants have the power
dog-men and their mean women
pulling poor blankets over
our sailors

(And where were you in our lean hour
Milking your moustache
or grinding a flower?)
I'm sick of dour faces
Staring at me from the TV
Tower, I want roses in
my garden bower; dig?
Royal babies, rubies
must now replace aborted
Strangers in the mud
These mutants, blood-meal
for the plant that's plowed

They are waiting to take us into
   the severed garden
Do you know how pale and wanton thrillful
   comes death on a strange hour
   unannounced, unplanned for
like a scaring over-friendly guest you've
   brought to bed
Death makes angels of us all
   and gives us wings
where we had shoulders
   smooth as raven's
     claws
No more money, no more fancy dress
This other Kingdom seems by far the best
until its other jaw reveals incest
and loose obedience to a vegetable law
I will not go
Prefer a Feast of Friends
To the Giant Family

*This verse, beginning with "We can invent . . . ," was not included on the recorded version.

INDEX OF SONG TITLES